Hypericum is the herb *Hypericum perforatum*, also known as St. John's wort (*wort* means "plant"). Hypericum has been used for thousands of years as a medicine.

In *Hypericum & Depression*, two noted psychiatrists report on the recent medical research that could change the way depression is treated in America. (In Germany, hypericum accounts for more than fifty percent of the antidepressant market. Prozac has two percent.)

In a simple, straightforward style, the authors explain what depression is, how know if one is depressed, the medical effects of hypericum on depression, and where to find research-grade hypericum (as not all hypericum supplements are alike).

Also included are summaries of selected medical studies on hypericum and depression.

If you know anyone who is depressed—or if you think you may be depressed yourself—this book is must reading.

HAROLD H. BLOOMFIELD, M.D., is a world-renowned Yale-trained psychiatrist. He has been in clinical practice for more than twenty-five years, specializing in the treatment of depression. His books—which have sold more than six million copies and have been translated into twenty-four languages—include *How to Heal Depression, How to Survive the Loss of a Love,* and *The Power of 5.* Dr. Bloomfield has a private practice in Del Mar, California.

MIKAEL NORDFORS, M.D., is a psychiatric researcher at Sahlgrehnska University Hospital in Gothenburg, Sweden. His medical knowledge, research skills, and fluency in several languages have been invaluable in tracking down, translating, and understanding the medical studies on hypericum.

PETER MCWILLIAMS is a writer and video author. His books include *How to Heal Depression* (with Dr. Bloomfield), *How to survive the Loss of a Love* (with Dr. Bloomfield and Melba Colgrove, Ph.D.), *You Can't Afford the Luxury of a Negative Thought, DO IT!* and *LIFE 101.*

St. John's wort is a promising treatment for depression .... Hypericum extracts were significantly superior to placebo and similarly effective as standard antidepressants .... The herb may offer an advantage, however, in terms of relative safety and tolerability, which might improve patient compliance.

—British Medical Journal
August 3, 1996

Move over, Prozac. German and American researchers report the herb known as St. John's wort may be effective in treating depression.

—TIME
August 12, 1996

Vital Cautions
(*Please* read these)

1. If you are having suicidal thoughts, and you think you even *may* act upon them, please get emergency medical help *at once*. Call a suicide hotline, your physician, your therapist, your religious counselor, or 911. Suicidal *thoughts* are a natural part of depression. Any plan to *act* on these thoughts is a danger signal that you must get help at once.

2. If you are taking prescription antidepressants, do not alter your dosage or combine with hypericum without first consulting your doctor. Do not take hypericum if you are taking an MAO inhibitor. (Please see the chapter, "For Those Currently Taking Prescription Antidepressants.")

3. If you have a preexisting medical or psychiatric condition, please consult your doctor before taking hypericum.

4. Although they are few and generally mild, you should carefully consider the side effects of hypericum before taking it. Please read the chapter, "The Side Effects of Hypericum."

PRELUDE PRESS

8159 Santa Monica Boulevard
Los Angeles, California 90046

800-LIFE-101 (800-543-3101)

Most of our books at Prelude Press are available for free browsing, downloading, or burning on the Internet:

http://www.mcwilliams.com

You might also enjoy the Internet site:

http://www.hypericum.com

Editor: Jean Sedillos

ISBN: 0-931580-36-6

Hypericum & Depression

Can Depression Be Successfully Treated with a Safe, Inexpensive, Medically Proven Herb Available without a Prescription?

Harold H. Bloomfield, M.D.
Mikael Nordfors, M.D.
& Peter McWilliams

Contents

Part Three:
Hypericum & Depression 57

Part Four: Medical Studies on Hypericum and Depression............ 95

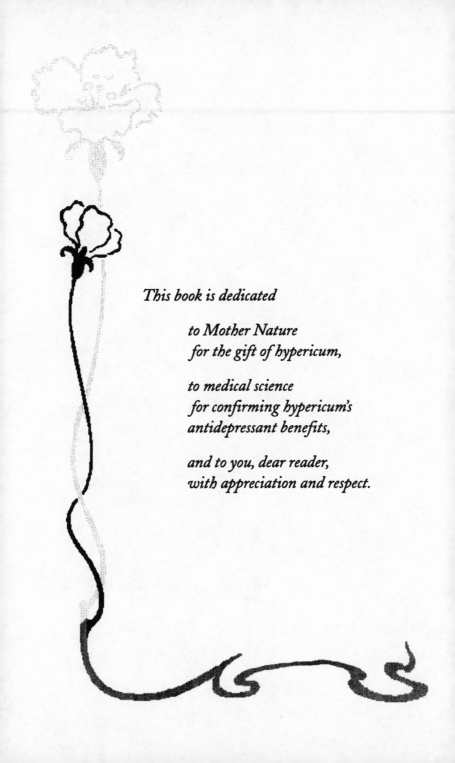

This book is dedicated

> *to Mother Nature*
> *for the gift of hypericum,*
>
> *to medical science*
> *for confirming hypericum's*
> *antidepressant benefits,*
>
> *and to you, dear reader,*
> *with appreciation and respect.*

Hypericum & Depression

Introduction

In 1993 while researching *How to Heal Depression*, we heard a great deal about natural treatments for depression. Everything from herbs (hypericum topping the list) to air (breathing exercises to ozone therapy) was recommended for healing depression.

Unfortunately, these claims were not then verified by extensive medical research. A study here or a study there may have been suggestive, but not enough to be considered fact. That didn't make the claims untrue, simply unproven.

In writing *How to Heal Depression*, however, we had no way, short of setting up a research institute, for separating the factual from the fanciful, so we chose to walk the scientifically proven straight-and-narrow.

That same year, more than a dozen medical studies on the effect of hypericum on depression were reaching completion. The results of these studies were remarkable:

The herb hypericum, in a significant number of people, relieved the symptoms of mild to moderate depression as effectively as prescription antidepressants. In addition, hypericum had virtually none of the negative side effects often associated with antidepressant medication.

All this from the extract of a flowering plant known since ancient times for its medicinal qualities—*Hypericum perforatum,* also known as St. John's wort. *(Wort,* by the way, means "plant.") Extracts of the plant are inexpensive and available without a prescription. Hypericum has fewer side effects than aspirin. Treatment costs about twenty-five cents a day.

In October 1994, the medically respected *Journal of Geriatric Psychiatry and Neurology* devoted its entire issue—seventeen scientific research papers in all—to "Hypericum: A Novel Antidepressant." Michael A. Jenike, M. D., editor, commented:

> The many studies form an impressive body of evidence indicating that hypericum may well be a potentially useful

agent to treat mild to moderate depressions. I have been impressed with the potential of the compound as a therapeutic agent in the treatment of mild to moderate depressive illnesses, the kind of depressions that predominate in outpatient medical practices. . . .

Antidepressant treatment with hypericum has been confirmed in multiple, double-blind scientific studies with similar effectiveness (50 to 80 percent) to synthetic antidepressant drugs. . . .

One major difference is that with hypericum side effects are rarely observed. Its mild side-effect profile may make it the first treatment-of-choice for mild to moderate depressions compared to the sexual dysfunction and other significant side effects of antidepressant drugs.

Hypericum's effectiveness in treating depression comes as good news to the mental health community. Physicians and therapists have a new tool to help patients, especially those who have not been helped by current antidepressant medications.

Traditionally, the health professional is an adjunct to the health care and preventative medicine practiced daily by the patient. What the patient cannot prevent or self-cure, the health care professional is called on to diagnose and treat. Until now, all forms of depression—even mild to moderate depression—required a diagnosis and a prescription from a physician.

But since the side effects of hypericum are mild and few (in one major study, less than 2.5 percent of the patients studied reported any adverse side effects at all), well-informed consumers might—after sufficient research—try hypericum as they would any other herb, vitamin, mineral, or over-the-counter medication. Hypericum thus allows the mental health professional to focus on those most seriously depressed.

Germany has been a world leader in researching hypericum. As a result, hypericum products account for more than fifty percent of the German antidepressant market. Prozac has less than two percent. Will the same revolution soon be taking place in America?

The excitement of discovering something new and useful absolutely requires (for us at any rate) telling others about it as soon as possible. And so we share this information with you in the best forum we know, a book.

With further study science will be able to chart more precisely the longitude and latitude of hypericum's usefulness in treating depression. With broader use and further investigation, side effects not yet attributed to hypericum may be discovered—especially in long-term use. Anyone considering taking hypericum should realize this and may want to contact his or her physician to discuss it.

One primary caution stands out: If you are currently taking prescription antidepressants, please do not change your dosage without your doctor's guidance. If you are taking a prescription antidepressant and suddenly stop, the "rebound effect" can be severe.

This book gives enough information for you to make—in consultation with your health care professional—an informed choice as to (a) whether you need treatment for depression, and (b) what that treatment might be.

With more research, the types of depression that can be successfully treated with hypericum may increase. For now, the twelve million Americans and 1.2 million Canadians who have mild to moderate depression but are not receiving proper treatment have a new, safe, and inexpensive treatment option.

A Note about Two Terms Used Often in This Book

Not surprisingly in a book entitled *Hypericum and Depression*, the two major terms we must define are *hypericum* and *depression*.

We have attempted to make this book as accessible to the general public as possible. Only in Part Four, "Medical Studies on Hypericum and Depression," aimed at healthcare professionals, are medical and scientific terms used without full explanation.

The first three parts of the book—"Depression," "Hypericum," and "Hypericum & Depression"— are as jargon-free as we know how to make them.

Hypericum in this book sometimes refers to the plant *Hypericum perforatum,* but most often it refers to the specific extract used in the majority of studies on the use of hypericum in treating depression. Not all hypericum extracts are alike, and only a few extracting methods and pharmaceutical forms have been subject to medical investigation. (Please see the chapter, "Obtaining Research-Grade Hypericum.")

When we use *depression,* we mean either dysthymia, or a major depression in the mild to moderate range, or to a combination of the two (the dreaded "double depression").

There are many types of depression: bipolar illness (manic-depression), seasonal affective disorder (SAD), postpartum depression, atypical depression, long-term low-grade depression (dysthymia), and major depression. (For a fuller explanation of the kinds of depression, please see our book, *How to Heal Depression.)*

Because most of the medical research to date has focused on the most prevalent forms of depression—mild to moderate major depression and dysthymia—when we use depression in this book, we refer to only these two. This does not mean hypericum would be ineffective in treating other forms of depression; it's just that the results are not in yet.

Medicine further describes the intensity of a major depression as either mild, moderate, or severe. The vast majority of major depressions fall in the mild-to-moderate range.

A depression must be clearly debilitating to be termed severe. Severe depression can include hallucinations and, in some cases, suicide attempts. It may require hospitalization.

Although even the most severe forms of depression can be successfully treated, often with rapid results, it is essential for seriously depressed people to receive proper medical supervision.

If a depression is experienced most of the day, more days than not, and continues for more than two years, it's known as *dysthymia. Thymia* comes from the Greek word *thumos,* meaning "mind" or "soul." *Dys* is the same as the prefix *dis*—it implies an imbalance, a negation. Any young person will tell you that "being dissed" is not a pleasant experience.

Dysthymia, then, is an imbalance, a negation, of the human mind and soul. It can start in childhood and continue well into adulthood. Left untreated, dysthymia can last an entire lifetime.

Fortunately, hypericum has been shown to be as effective as prescription antidepressants in treating both mild to moderate major depression and dysthymia.

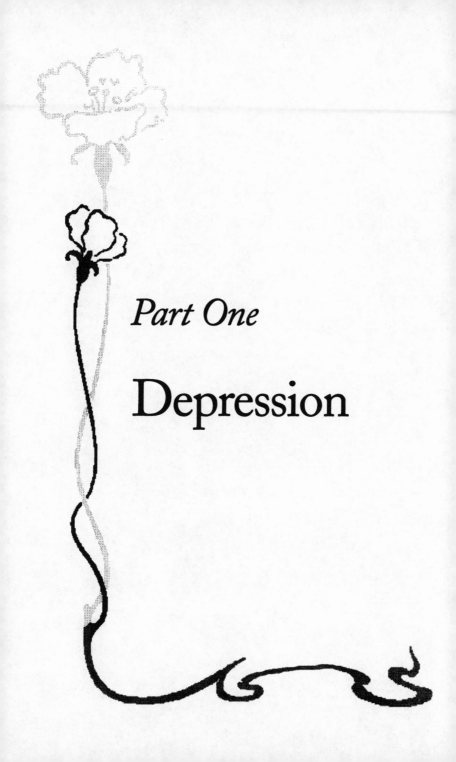

Part One

Depression

What Is Depression?

Depression is a medical illness, an illness with symptoms and a proven course of medical treatment that is effective in more than eighty percent of the cases.

Depression is more than just the occasional bad mood. It is not the natural mourning that takes place after a loss, or the "downs" in life's ordinary cycle of ups-and-downs.

Depression can be difficult to diagnose or to recognize in oneself. The symptoms of depression easily hide behind the ordinary experience of life.

Just a glance at the National Institutes of Health's symptoms of depression checklist reveals that depression overlaps normal, healthy living at many points.

According to the National Institutes of Health, the Symptoms of Depression can Include:

◉ Persistent sad or "empty" mood

◉ Loss of pleasure in ordinary activities, including sex

◉ Decreased energy, fatigue, being "slowed down"

◉ Sleep disturbances (insomnia, early-morning wakening, or oversleeping)

◉ Eating disturbances (loss of appetite and weight, or weight gain)

◉ Feelings of guilt, worthlessness, helplessness

◉ Thoughts of death or suicide, suicide attempts

◉ Irritability

◉ Excessive crying

◉ Chronic aches and pains that don't respond to treatment

In the Workplace, the Symptoms of Depression Often May Be Recognized by:

⚙ Decreased productivity

⚙ Morale problems

⚙ Lack of cooperation

⚙ Safety problems, accidents

⚙ Absenteeism

⚙ Frequent complaints of being tired all the time

⚙ Complaints of unexplained aches and pains

⚙ Alcohol and drug abuse

Healthy people, of course, regularly experience one or more of these symptoms. At what point, then, do ordinary "downs" become depression?

We must look first at intensity. How intense is the symptom? Hardly noticeable or overwhelming? If any one symptom significantly interferes with friends, family, or work, it can indicate depression.

We must also look at duration. How long have the

symptoms been going on? If one has not felt pleasure for an hour, that would not indicate depression. If, on the other hand, one has not felt pleasure for a month, depression (or some other imbalance, perhaps physical) may be indicated.

Finally, one must consider the number of symptoms. Many people don't know they have a depression because they experience their symptoms intermittently or at low levels. While none of the symptoms stand out enough to seek medical help, the collective symptoms of depression drain the psyche of the ability to enjoy life.

The National Institutes of Health, therefore, recommends:

> A thorough diagnosis is needed if four or more of the symptoms of depression persist for more than two weeks, or are interfering with work or family life.

Because the symptoms of depression are so close to home, and because we human beings are such masters of self-deception and denial, it's difficult to objectively evaluate oneself for depression.

Anne Hedonia

Many people mistakenly dismiss depression because they are not unduly troubled by the actively negative aspects of depression—pain, insomnia, guilt, anxiety, and so on. One may have none of these overtly negative symptoms and still be depressed.

Depression also manifests itself by a lack of positives. Many people experience depression as a lack of pleasure rather than as the presence of pain.

The lack of pleasure as a symptom of depression is known medically as *anhedonia—an* meaning "not" and *hedonia* meaning "pleasure."

Anhedonia is the inability to experience pleasure—or even true contentment—for any significant period of time.

The original title for Woody Allen's film *Annie Hall* was *Anne Hedonia*. Although he changed the title of the film, anhedonia remains the perfect description of Woody Allen's character in almost all his films—a person who, for the most part, is not enjoying life.

Woody Allen began *Annie Hall* with a joke from a 1919 Fanny Brice monologue:

> Two elderly women are in a Catskill Mountain resort and one of them says, "Boy, the food in this place is really terrible."
>
> The other one says, "Yeah, I know, and such small portions."
>
> That's essentially how I feel about life.

And a perfect description of anhedonia.

The Undertreatment of Depression

Depression is one of the most undertreated medical illnesses in this country. It is estimated that twelve million people in the United States and 1.2 million in Canada suffer from depression and do not know it. Because depression can so often be successfully treated, most of this suffering is unnecessary.

Some of the reasons for this underdiagnosis and undertreatment were mentioned earlier, but bear repeating and elaboration here.

First, it's easy to find a cause other than depression to explain away—to oneself or others—depression's symptoms. Hence, the true cause of these imbalances—depression—is not considered.

Second, when considering medical treatment, people tend to look for negative symptoms—pain or discomfort. The notion that "lack of pleasure" might be the symptom of an illness needing medical treatment seldom occurs. If the thought, "I'm not enjoying myself enough," does occur, it is often disregarded by the depressed person—or by well-meaning but unknowing friends—as trivial or self-indulgent.

Many people justify their increasingly unpleasant lives by saying, "It's just a phase," "I've been under a lot of pressure lately," or "I must be getting older."

But that is often not the case. Each year more than 30,000 people commit suicide in the United States. Fully seventy percent of these suicides were due to untreated depression. Left untreated, depression's burden of a joyless life accumulates, day by day, month by month, year by year. Depression can become a life-threatening illness.

Third, depression has symptoms people seldom associate with "being depressed." Unfortunately, the term *depressed* has taken on two meanings— the medical meaning we have been discussing in this book, and the everyday usage of *depression:*

momentary disappointment, letdown, or discontent. "The 7-11 ran out of glazed donuts. I'm so depressed."

Depression, then, is thought of by many as simply feeling low or down. The illness of depression, many people have inaccurately concluded, must be feeling very low and very down. If these people don't feel very low or very down very often, they dismiss the possibility of depression.

Certainly some of the symptoms of a depressive illness are feeling low or down, but one can have a mild to moderate depression without feeling "depressed" much at all.

Such symptoms as sleep disturbance; eating disorders; difficulty concentrating, remembering, or making decisions; drug or alcohol abuse; and especially physical aches and pains are not directly associated with emotionally feeling low, but they can be symptoms of medical depression.

Finally, some people who think they might have a depression do not seek treatment because they feel anxious over, angry about, or undeserving of a cure. In these cases, the very symptoms of the disease keep the disease from being treated.

The Treatment of Depression

In addition to hypericum, which we will discuss shortly, there are two medically proven methods of treating depression: (a) two specific forms of "talk" therapy and (b) antidepressant medication.

The talk therapies are Cognitive Therapy and Interpersonal Therapy. They are short-term, usually less than twenty one-hour sessions. Both involve the therapist working with the client in reshaping the client's thinking, perceptions, and view of the world so that they better serve the client.

These therapies rely on the fact that if one's view—one's cognition—of the world, relationships, and oneself is made less depressing, then one tends to feel less depressed.

Some people have never learned to see the world, themselves, and their relationships in anything but depressing terms. Cognitive and Interpersonal therapies aim at teaching a person how to live more reasonably, joyfully, and productively.

Even though the focus of this book is treating depression with hypericum, please do not conclude that we do not enthusiastically support and recommend Cognitive Therapy and Interpersonal Therapy, because we do.

The second form of treatment is antidepressant medication. In the past few decades, antidepressant medications have dramatically changed the way in which depression is treated.

Antidepressants work on the generally accepted medical theory that depressed people have a biochemical imbalance, which is sometimes genetic. This internal biological imbalance causes the brain to function at less than optimum levels. It is this biochemical imbalance that leads to the mental, emotional, and physical ramifications known as depression.

The human brain is the most intricate, complex, and exquisite communication center on earth. Ten billion brain cells transmit billions of messages each second. And, as Alan Watts pointed out, "It does all this without our even thinking about it." The biochemical messengers of this communication are known as *neurotransmitters*. *(Neuro* refers to the brain cells and *transmitter* to sending and receiving information.)

When neurotransmitters are at appropriate levels, the brain functions harmoniously. We tend to feel good. We have hope, purpose, and direction. Although we certainly experience the ups and downs of life, the overall mood is one of well-being, confidence, and security.

Research indicates that a deficiency in some of the neurotransmitters may be one cause of depression. On the other hand, excess amounts of neurotransmitters may be a cause of the manic phase of manic-depression.

Restoring these neurotransmitters to natural levels by way of antidepressant medication brings the brain back into harmonious functioning and a return to well-being.

The biochemical imbalance known as depression is not cured, but it can be successfully treated for as long as the depressive illness persists. (For some people, it will be the rest of their lives.)

Unfortunately, antidepressant medications have

gotten some undeserved bad press. Antidepressant medications, taken under medical supervision, are among the safest of prescription medications.

There are side effects to antidepressant medications, just as there are side effects to all prescriptive medications. (That's one of the reasons they require a prescription.) Roughly half the people who take antidepressant medications, however, experience no side effects at all.

The side effects of prescription antidepressants include decreased sexual desire or function, dry mouth, nausea, tiredness, restlessness, and negative interactions with alcohol or other drugs.

Different antidepressant medications have different side effects in different individuals. If an unpleasant side effect is experienced with antidepressant A, antidepressants B, C, D, E, and more are still available to treat the depression.

More than seven million people in the United States are successfully being treated with antidepressant medications. Thanks to antidepressants, these seven million live happier, healthier, more productive lives.

The Difficulty in Treating Depression

Although the strides in treating depression have been remarkable, public acceptance of depression as an illness—with specific symptoms and a high rate of successful treatment—has not been as dramatic.

As we have explored, many people with depression do not get treatment because they do not recognize what they have is an illness. If people don't know they have an illness, they don't tend to seek help for it.

Depression is often diagnosed in people who have not sought help for it, but have consulted a health care professional for one of depression's many symptoms, such as insomnia, fatigue, aches and pains, or overeating.

Failure to seek treatment is the first—and largest—hurdle in treating depression.

Another hurdle for many is expense. All antidepressant medications require a prescription. A prescription requires a diagnosis, which requires a physician, which requires (usually) money.

Also, the cost of the latest antidepressant medications can be as high as seven dollars per day. To many, this extra two-hundred and twenty dollars a month is an impossible expense.

Finally, there is the tendency—normal in most people but exaggerated in those with depression—not to make changes and not to try new things. The thought of going to a doctor and saying, "I'm not feeling a lot of pleasure. I think I need medication," seems strange to most people, so they don't seek help.

If the depression cures itself (as it can), the person feels vindicated in waiting. But what about the quality of life during the depression? And what will the person do if the depression returns?

Once a patient sees a physician and is diagnosed as having depression, the treatment begins. Treatment of depression is as much an art as it is a science.

If the treatment is based on antidepressant medications, choosing the right medication for the patient is essential. Unfortunately, the choice is not always clear.

There is no way of knowing, for example, which side effects might appear in which patient taking which medication. The physician prescribes an antidepressant with the fewest side effects and relies on the patient to report the results.

Alas, the side effects of antidepressant medications have caused a good number of people to abandon the treatment of depression altogether.

Another difficulty in prescribing antidepressants is that the optimum dose and timing (how many milligrams of medication how many times per day taken how many hours apart) for antidepressants vary greatly from patient to patient.

Finding the right antidepressant for a patient is a matter of trial and error—although most physicians prefer to call it "art."

This trial-and-error procedure—perfectly acceptable and sometimes necessary in medical treatment—is made more difficult because antidepressant medications can take several weeks to take full effect.

Unlike, say, a pain pill, with which the effectiveness can be determined within a couple of hours, it takes as long as six weeks before one can declare a given antidepressant ineffective.

Further, many of the side effects of prescriptive antidepressants may be severe at first, but can become less and even disappear entirely over time.

These two factors can lead to a months-long (but ultimately worthwhile) quest for the proper antidepressant. As we shall see, using hypericum to treat depression bypasses most of these problems.

One should not think in terms of prescription antidepressants *versus* hypericum. There is no battle between them. Hypericum is simply a new and medically proven tool for treating depression, a tool that joins prescription antidepressants in the health care professional's arsenal for combating illness, pain, and suffering.

That's where the real battle lies.

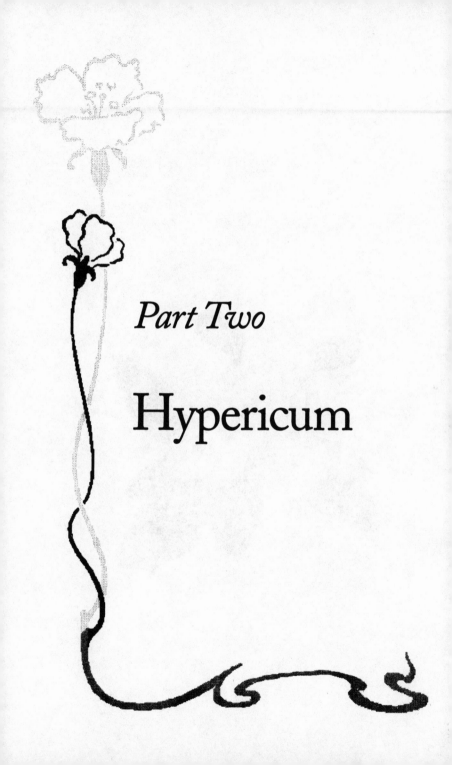

Part Two

Hypericum

Hypericum Perforatum

Hypericum's complete botanical name is *Hypericum perforatum.*

Perforatum is Latin for "perforated." The leaves of *Hypericum perforatum,* when held to the light, reveal translucent dots, giving the impression that the leaf is perforated. The dots are not holes in the leaf, but a layer of colorless essential plant oils and resin.

The flowers are a bright yellow-orange. The petals are peppered with black dots. When the black dots are rubbed between the fingers, the fingers become red.

Many herbalists say the translucent "perforations" and the black-red spots contain the most active medicinal qualities.

The stem of *Hypericum perforatum* is unique. As Rudolf Fritz Weiss, M.D., describes it in his book *Herbal Medicine:*

> The plant has two raised lines down the stem. This is something quite unusual in the plant world. Round or four-square stems are the general rule. It is only *H. perforatum* which has these two raised lines, making the stem appear pressed flat.

Hypericum perforatum is also known as St. John's wort. (As previously stated, *wort* means "plant.") How the *Hypericum perforatum* wort got to be named after St. John is not known. Like most unknown things, however, the naming of St. John's wort has a number of perfectly reasonable, possibly even true, explanations.

All seem to agree that the plant's namesake was John the Baptist, not John the Beloved. The stories as to why *Hypericum perforatum* was named after the baptizer include:

> ● When the Bible says John lived on locusts and wild honey, the Greek word for

locusts might have meant not just the insects, but the tops of plants on which the locusts alight. (The Greek word *akron* is an image of a locust landing on the top of a plant.) Usually in the Bible *akron* means the bug, but legend has it that when it refers to John the Baptist's culinary delights, the word includes both insect and plant.

The legend takes a locust-sized leap in assuming the plant St. John may have ingested with his honey-coated insects was *Hypericum perforatum*. But if that legend does not hold up to logical investigation, there are others.

● The black-red spots on the petals represent the blood shed by John at his beheading, and the translucent spots on the leaves represent the tears shed over that event.

● *Hypericum perforatum*, a plant which grows wild (it's considered a troublesome weed in Colorado and Australia), blooms in summer. This corresponds to the celebration of St. John's Tide. The hypericum flowers, which can cover a field in brilliant yellow blooms, were called St. John's wort because they appeared around St. John's Tide.

⊛ Maybe all three.

⊛ Maybe none.

Whatever the reason for its name, by medieval times people believed that if you slept with a sprig of St. John's wort under your pillow on St. John's Eve (the night before St. John's Tide),

> the Saint would appear in a dream, give
> his blessing, and prevent one from dying
> during the following year.

Hypericum perforatum has a long service to human-kind—some decorative (it makes excellent ground cover) and some medicinal.

Hypericum as Medicine

In his book *The Healing Power of Herbs*, Michael T. Murray, N.D., pointed out:

> St. John's wort has a long history of folk use. Dioscorides, the foremost physician of ancient Greece, as well as Pliny [in ancient Rome] and Hippocrates [the father of medicine], administered St. John's wort in the treatment of many illnesses.
>
> Its Latin name, *Hypericum perforatum,* is derived from Greek and means "over an apparition," a reference to the belief that

the herb was so obnoxious to evil spirits
that a whiff of it would cause them to
depart.

In folk medicine, St. John's wort has been used in the treatment of wounds (it has powerful antibacterial and antiviral properties), kidney and lung ailments, and what we would now call depression.

Rodale's Illustrated Encyclopedia of Herbs reports:

> The herb is said to soothe the digestive system. In particular, its ingredients were thought to relieve ulcers and gastritis, and the herb was called on as a folk medicine for diarrhea and nausea. Bruises and hemorrhoids are said to respond to it. It has served as a sedative, painkiller, and analgesic. The blossoms have been added to sweek oil (a refined olive oil used medicinally) for a soothing dressing for cuts. Herbalists credit it with increasing and inducing a sense of well-being.

Long before depression was isolated as an illness by traditional western medicine, the symptoms of depression—worry, "nervous unrest," sleep disturbances, and others—were treated in folk medicine by St. John's wort.

In modern herbal medicine, St. John's wort is used

first and foremost to treat depression. If you sought the guidance of an herbalist for the treatment of depression, the herbalist would almost invariably recommend hypericum first.

As the medical studies on hypericum become better known to health care professionals, the use of hypericum may become the first line of treatment in traditional western medicine as well.

Hypericum is currently being medically studied as a treatment for AIDS, several forms of cancer, bed wetting and night terrors in children, skin diseases such as psoriasis, rheumatoid arthritis, peptic ulcers, and even hangover. (Hypericum mixes with and keeps well in alcohol. Who knows how long before hypericum is added to alcoholic beverages and then hailed as hangover-reduced alcohol?)

From the viewpoint of traditional western medicine, we seem only at the threshold of hypericum's proven usefulness.

Part Three

Hypericum
& Depression

The Good News

Now that we've covered the basics, we can discuss the good news about hypericum and depression.

In a nutshell: Medical research has shown that hypericum is an effective treatment for depression—as successful as prescription antidepressants in the majority of patients.

The medical studies show that from fifty to eighty percent of depressed patients have a significant decrease in the symptoms of depression and a corresponding increase in well-being. This success rate is the same as that of prescription antidepressants.

Unlike prescription antidepressants, however, (a) the side effects of hypericum are few and mild, (b) hypericum costs considerably less, and (c) hypericum is available without a prescription.

Hypericum opens whole new avenues of treatment for the eighteen million people in this country who have depression—especially the twelve million who are not currently receiving any treatment whatsoever.

Hypericum is the most extensively researched and used herbal antidepressant known. Over 5,000 patients have participated in drug-monitoring studies—more than 2,000 of these in double-blind studies. Eight head-to-head comparisons showed hypericum was as effective as prescription antidepressants, but with fewer side effects. More than twenty million people in Germany regularly take hypericum for depression.

The high success rate of treatment—combined with hypericum's minimal side effects, low cost, and availability—make hypericum, for many people, the first line of treatment for long-term low-grade depression and for mild to moderate major depression.

This section of the book explores this good news. Let's begin by exploring the side effects of hypericum.

The Side Effects of Hypericum

St. John's wort has an excellent safety record during centuries of folk medicine. Recent medical studies confirm this safety. The extensive use of hypericum in Germany (sixty-six million daily doses in 1994) has not resulted in medical reports of serious drug interactions or even toxicity after accidental overdose.

No substance is perfectly safe. Indeed, substances which are essential to human life are, when ingested in sufficient quantities, very harmful. Hence the warning label on all over-the-counter medications: "Safe when used as directed." Even common table salt—a necessary mineral to human existence—is deadly when taken in excess.

In exploring side effects, one must compare the relative dangers—how toxic is one substance as compared to another? Aspirin is less toxic than morphine but more toxic than, say, vitamin C.

One must also compare the dangers with the relative benefits. One must weigh the damage caused by the illness with the potential damage caused by the treatment. Chemotherapy involves some of the most toxic chemicals known to medicine but when compared to not using these chemicals—death by cancer—they become medically acceptable.

In both categories, hypericum is impressive.

As to toxicity, hypericum is safer than aspirin. Five hundred to one thousand people die each year in the United States from aspirin, usually from internal bleeding. Hypericum, by comparison, does not have a single recorded human death in 2,400 years of known medicinal use.

In fact, the only fatal toxicity known is in certain light-skinned animals, such a sheep, who die not from ingesting large quantities of St. John's wort while grazing, but of exposure to sun after. (This is why hypericum is considered a dangerous weed in Australia and is listed in *Common Poisonous Plants and Mushrooms of North America,* by Nancy J. Turner and Adam F. Szczawinski.) Hypericum increases the animals' susceptibility to sunlight, and they become sick and sometimes die from extreme sunburn. Medically, it's known as *phototoxicity*—the overexposure to light *(photo)* is harmful *(toxic)*.

This phenomenon, while theoretically possible in humans, has not been documented in the recommended doses for depression. Not a single case of phototoxicity has been reported in human medical studies at depression-dosage levels. Even in AIDS research involving intravenous hypericum doses thirty-five times greater than the recommended dose for depression, the phototoxic effects have been few and never deadly. (High doses of hypericum are being medically investigated for its antiviral properties.)

The potential for phototoxicity should be kept in mind, however, if one has a prior hypersensitivity to sunlight, or if one is taking other photosensitizing drugs such as Chlorpromazine and Tetracyclines.

In a study of 3,250 patients taking hypericum,

only 2.4 percent experienced any side effects at all.

The side effects reported tended to be mild. Gastrointestinal irritations accounted for 0.6 percent, allergic reactions for 0.5 percent, tiredness for 0.4 percent, and restlessness for 0.3 percent.

(Interestingly, in fifteen studies involving 1,008 patients, the side effects in the control group given a harmless placebo were slightly higher than that of hypericum—4.8 percent for the placebo group and 4.1 percent for hypericum. The dropout rate of the placebo group was higher, too—1.8 percent for the placebo group compared with 0.4 percent for hypericum.)

A higher figure was reported by the *British Medical Journal* in a review of six hypericum studies. In these, 10.8 percent of the patients reported side effects with hypericum (similar to the ones listed above), while 35.9 percent reported side effects taking prescription antidepressants. Even at this higher rate, the *British Medical Journal* concluded the side effects of hypericum were "rare and mild."

The *British Medical Journal* also calls for more studies on the long-term potential side effects of hypericum, a recommendation we wholehearted endorse. We can, however, consider facts that lie outside the strict standards of medical reporting.

For example, the extensive use of St. John's wort in 2,400 years of folk and herbal medicine as well as the twenty-million people in Germany who have been taking hypericum for more than a year and have not reported any long-term side effects different or more prevalent than those of the shorter-term medical studies.

Some of the most troublesome side effects of prescription antidepressants—reduced sexual drive or dysfunction, adverse interaction with alcohol or other drugs, dry mouth, and headache—were not reported by patients taking hypericum.

Further, hypericum's side effects went away soon after the patients stopped taking it. There were no "nonreversible" side effects; that is, no permanent harm was done and all side effects were quickly reversed as soon as the patients no longer took hypericum.

The side effects of hypericum are mild, indeed, when compared to the symptoms of depression. At the extreme are the 21,000 suicides (70 percent of all suicides) that are a direct result of untreated depression. Studies have shown that for every suicide there are ten unsuccessful suicide attempts and one hundred people who are seriously contemplating suicide.

Untreated depression is the number-one cause of alcoholism, drug abuse, eating disorders, and other addictions. A significant percentage of divorces, spousal and child abuse, absenteeism from work, lost jobs, and bankruptcies are attributed to untreated depression.

It is estimated that losses associated with depression in the United States amount to more than forty billion dollars each year. And who can put a price on the daily suffering of the twelve million Americans and 1.2 million Canadians who have depression but are not being treated?

Compared with the symptoms of depression, the side effects of hypericum seem insignificant. For most people suffering symptoms of depression, the potential benefits far outweigh the possible risk of taking hypericum.

The low side-effect profile of hypericum—especially when taken in the dosage recommended for the treatment of depression—puts it in the category of herbs, vitamins, minerals, and over-the-counter medications.

Ever watchful for potential side effects, well-informed consumers can take hypericum with confidence.

The Recommended Dosage of Hypericum

The optimum dosage of hypericum, based on the majority of medical studies, is 300 mg of hypericum extract containing 0.3 percent hypericin (an active ingredient of hypericum) three times a day. This 300 mg dosage fits comfortably into a single tablet or capsule.

Some find one with each meal—breakfast, lunch, and dinner—is a convenient and effective way to take hypericum. Some find that taking two 300 mg doses at breakfast and a third at lunch or dinner works best.

Because hypericum is tolerated so well by the body, experimentation with dosage and timing has far fewer risks than experimentation with most prescription medications.

As the side effects of hypericum are few even in significantly higher doses, one can, for example, take four 250 mg capsules daily if only 250 mg capsules are available.

Small children should take a total of 300 mg of hypericum daily, while larger children should take 600 mg per day. For adolescents, the full adult dose is recommended.

Hypericum's effectiveness in treating depression should not be evaluated until at least six weeks of a 900 mg daily antidepressant dose. As with prescription antidepressants, the effect of hypericum takes place gradually. Studies generally indicate that hypericum takes longer to reach full effectiveness than do prescription antidepressants.

One should not be too anxious for an immediate "cure," as one might expect from aspirin or a decongestant. The best course is to be watchful for possible side effects, take hypericum "as directed," and make an objective evaluation of benefits six weeks after starting.

It is important to give hypericum a chance. To decide after one or two weeks, "This isn't working for me," and discontinue treatment is ill advised.

Certainly if side effects occur, you should consult your healthcare provider. Often the side effects of hypericum—especially milder side effects—disappear on their own as the body becomes accustomed to the hypericum. Sometimes a slight reduction of the dosage is called for while the body adjusts.

If the symptoms are severe, stop taking hypericum at once and contact your healthcare professional. All symptoms should fade entirely within a few days after you stop.

If the side effects of depression become worse or you are having suicidal impulses, please see your doctor immediately.

After six weeks, one might decide to take slightly more or slightly less hypericum, depending on the results. Hypericum is not a "more is better" herb. The goal is alleviating the symptoms of depression. For most people, this is accomplished with three 300 mg doses per day.

If a satisfactory effect is not achieved in six weeks, one should consult with a physician and discuss taking a prescription antidepressant instead. Like hypericum, prescription antidepressants are not "uppers," stimulants, or addictive.

Depression must be treated. Even with their greater cost and higher side-effect profile, if prescription antidepressants are necessary to successfully treat a depression, they should be taken.

There are many prescription antidepressants to choose from. If one is not successful in treating depression, or if the side effects are severe, there are several others from which to choose. Please work with your doctor to find the prescription antidepressant that is right for you.

The Young, the Elderly, and the Physically Ill

Two percent of all children and five percent of adolescents suffer from depression. People over sixty-five and those chronically or severely ill are more likely to suffer depression than the general population.

Unfortunately, these people often have less tolerance for the side effects of prescription antidepressants, or find that prescription antidepressants may adversely interact with medication they are already taking. And then there's the cost.

For these groups especially, hypericum comes as a godsend. Its few side effects, apparent noninteraction with other medications, and relatively low cost make hypericum an ideal choice for alleviating the symptoms of depression for the young, the old, and the ill.

One must be especially cautious when giving prescription medication to children. The still-developing nervous system needs all the protection it can get. This is why physicians are often more hesitant to prescribe antidepressants for children. With hypericum, this concern is far less.

In the young and in the elderly, depression often goes untreated because of the standard justifications, "It's just a phase" (for young people) and "That's just part of getting older" (for older people). If the "phase" continues for more than two weeks, depression should be considered.

"Just getting older" should never include the symptoms of depression on an ongoing basis. As the editor of the *Journal of Geriatric Psychiatry and Neurology*, Michael Jenike, M.D., reported:

> The benign side-effect profile may make hypericum a particularly attractive choice for treating mild to moderate depression in our elderly patients.

In the ill, the symptoms of depression often overlap the symptoms of the physical illness—fatigue, aches and pains, confusion, anxiety, and others. Rather than dismiss these as "just part of being sick," depression should be considered. Indeed, serious illness can trigger a depression, so depression should especially be considered if one is not well physically.

For Those Currently Taking Prescription Antidepressants

If one is successfully being treated with prescription antidepressants, there are no adverse side effects, and the cost is not a prohibitive factor, the first question to ask is, "Why change?"

We have no good reasons. As we've already discussed, the treatment of depression is as much an art as a science, and where the art and science of medicine have combined to successfully treat an illness, one should interfere only for good reason.

Those, however, who are currently taking prescription antidepressants and want to switch to hypericum must observe certain safeguards.

Alas, the medical research on switching from prescription antidepressants to hypericum is virtually nonexistent. From what is known about hypericum and prescription antidepressants, certain guidelines can be established.

> 1. Do not stop taking prescription antidepressants without proper medical care. The "rebound effect" of stopping prescription antidepressants too abruptly can be severe.

> 2. Do not take hypericum for severe depression or bipolar (manic-depressive) illness. Not enough research has been done on hypericum and these types of depression. As we've said, the vast majority of depressions fall in the mild to moderate range. A depression must be clearly debilitating to be termed severe. Severe depression can include hallucinations and, in some cases, suicide attempts. It may require hospitalization. The physician who prescribed the antidepressants or who is currently monitoring the course of treatment is the best person to determine whether one is severely depressed.

3. Do not take hypericum while taking mono-amino-oxidase (MAO) inhibitors such as Nardil or Parnate. It appears that hypericum works at least in part as a serotonin reuptake inhibitor (SRI). Combining an SRI with an MAO inhibitor can produce a dangerous rise in blood pressure. After stopping MAO inhibitors, one should wait four weeks before taking any SRIs—prescription or hypericum. This caution, however, is not based on specific medical research on hypericum and MAO inhibitors, but on what is known about prescription SRIs and MAO inhibitors. Until further research is done on how and why hypericum works to alleviate the symptoms of depression, hypericum should be considered an SRI and treated accordingly.

The best way to make the transition to hypericum from SRIs—Prozac, Paxil, Zoloft, and Effexor—is not known. Medical studies exploring this question are sorely needed.

If hypericum acts as a serotonin reuptake inhibitor in the same way as prescription SRIs, then it would appear that a gradual introduction of hypericum while tapering off the prescription antidepressant would be in order.

Hypericum tends to take longer to reach maximum effect in the body than do prescription antidepressants. This may indicate that a gradual building up of hypericum over four to six weeks should precede a significant reduction in the prescription antidepressants.

One must at the same time be careful not to take too many SRIs, to avoid the medical condition known as *serotonin syndrome*. Here the brain has too much serotonin—the opposite of what happens in depression—and symptoms include sweating, agitation, confusion, lethargy, tremor, and muscle jerks. If such symptoms occur, consult your doctor immediately.

Of course, the possibility always exists that the hypericum may not treat the depression as successfully as the prescription antidepressant. It should not and cannot be assumed, just because one found successful treatment with prescription antidepressants, that hypericum will prove equally successful. A certain percentage of people will not respond to hypericum as well as they responded to prescription antidepressants.

It is reassuring, however, to know that the side effects of hypericum are few and hypericum's negative interaction with any other drug (other than, potentially, MAO inhibitors) has not been reported.

As research continues, we will attempt to keep current on the best methods of making the transition from prescription antidepressants and print them in future editions of this book.

We will also update this chapter on the Internet version of this book, available at no cost at:

http://www.hypericum.com

How to Obtain Research-Grade Hypericum

Unlike prescription or generic drugs, herbal preparations are sold in a variety of formulations and methods of extraction. When you buy aspirin, you know you're getting aspirin, no matter which brand name you buy. When you buy hypericum or St. John's wort, you don't know exactly what you're getting.

A company can grind up the dried *Hypericum perforatum* plant, put it into capsules, and quite rightly call it "hypericum" or "St. John's wort." This is, however, not the method of preparation for the research-grade hypericum used in the majority of medical studies on hypericum and depression. In time, medical research may show that ground-up *Hypericum perforatum* is just as effective in treating depression as other methods of extraction. As of now, however, only one method of preparation has been medically proven to be successful.

The method, briefly, is to take the flowering and leafy portions of the *Hypericum perforatum* plant, dry them, and use alcohol to dissolve the useful elements from the plant. When the alcohol evaporates, the extract remains. The extract is then tested and adjusted so that the hypericin (one of hypericum's active ingredients) concentration is 0.3 percent. This method is generally known as *alcohol extraction*. There is no alcohol in the finished product, but alcohol is necessary to extract the medically useful chemicals from the plant.

With *Hypericum perforatum,* the chemicals believed to be most useful for the treatment of depression are obtained through alcohol extraction. This is why a tea made from St. John's wort ("water extraction") may not be as effective. No studies have been performed to explore the effectiveness of hypericum tea on depression. (The medicinal chemicals of *Hypericum perforatum* also dissolve well in oil, hence the herbal medicine olive-oil-based preparations for treating external injuries.)

Of the many chemicals known to exist naturally in *Hypericum perforatum*, it is not yet known precisely which—or which combination—is responsible for the successful treatment of depression. Future medical studies may isolate which of these chemicals and in what combination most successfully treat depression.

Until that time, those seeking to duplicate the success of the medical studies reported in this book are advised to use the same extract formulation used in the majority of those studies.

Fortunately, this formulation is available under a number of brand names in the United States and Canada, sold both by mail and through retail outlets. With the increased interest in treating depression with hypericum, the number of products will rise and we will include them in future printings of this book. Also, this chapter will be updated in the Internet version of this book, which is available at

http://www.hypericum.com

Here are the trade names of the available *Hypericum perforatum* extracts that our research has shown contain the same formulation used in much of the medical research on hypericum and depression (listed in order of value):

PRODUCT NAME: Hypericum Verbatim
COMPANY: Hypericum Buyer's Club
STRENGTH: 300 mg
TYPE: Scored tablet (breaks into two 150 mg doses for children or for adjusting an adult dose; no animal products used)
COST: $27.50 for 280 tablets
COST PER DAY: **29 cents (best value by far)**
AVAILABLE: Mail order
MAIL ORDER ADDRESS: Hypericum Buyer's Club, 8205 Santa Monica Boulevard, Suite 472, Los Angeles, California 90046
MAIL ORDER TELEPHONE: 888-HYPERICUM (888-497-3742), 24 hours
SHIPPING & HANDLING CHARGE: None

❁

PRODUCT NAME: St. John's Wort
COMPANY: Solaray
STRENGTH: 300 mg
TYPE: Gelatin capsule
COST: $9.05 for 60 capsules
COST PER DAY: **60 cents (by mail)**
AVAILABLE: Health food stores; mail order
MAIL ORDER TELEPHONE: 800-447-6527
SHIPPING & HANDLING CHARGE: $3.00

NOTE: Solaray sells four St. John's wort formulations. The one that matches the extract used in the medical studies is labeled "Guaranteed Potency" and is 300 mg (not 250 or 325 mg). And no matter what they may say, three (not one) 300 mg tablets is the daily dose.

❀

PRODUCT NAME: St. John's Wort
COMPANY: Enzymatic Therapy
STRENGTH: 300 mg
TYPE: Gelatin capsule
COST: $12.95 for 60 capsules
COST PER DAY: **65 cents**
AVAILABLE: Health food stores

❀

PRODUCT NAME: St. John's Wort Whole Extract
COMPANY: Elixir Tonics & Teas
STRENGTH: 300 mg
TYPE: Vegi-cap capsules (no animal products)
COST: $16.95 for 90 capsules
COST PER DAY: **70 cents (by mail)**
AVAILABLE: Elixir's retail store or by mail
MAIL ORDER & STORE ADDRESS: 8612 Melrose Avenue, West Hollywood, California 90069
MAIL ORDER TELEPHONE: 888-4TONICS
SHIPPING & HANDLING CHARGE: $4.00

❀

PRODUCT NAME: St. John's Wort
COMPANY: Nature's Sunshine
STRENGTH: 300 mg
TYPE: Gelatin capsule
COST: $26.40 for 100 capsules
COST PER DAY: **79 cents**
AVAILABLE: Multi-level marketing. Call for your local representative: 800-223-8225.

❋

PRODUCT NAME: St. John's Wort
COMPANY: Nature's Resources
STRENGTH: 150 mg (6 PER DAY NEEDED)
TYPE: Gelatin capsule
COST: $7.39 for 50 capsules
COST PER DAY: **87 cents**
AVAILABLE: Drug stores; mass merchandisers

❋

PRODUCT NAME: Kira
COMPANY: Lichtwer Pharma U.S., Inc.
STRENGTH: 300 mg
TYPE: Tablet
COST: $15.99 for 45 capsules
COST PER DAY: **$1.06 cents**
AVAILABLE: Drug stores; mass merchandisers

Hypericum, Herbs, and Health Policy

We turn this chapter over to an expert in the field of law and nutritional supplements, Mary Elizabeth Conn, J.D., M.B.A. She is an Assistant Professor of Business Law at the University of San Diego and has a private practice as a trial attorney. She is currently serving as Special Deputy Trial Counsel for the State Bar of California.

We are grateful to Professor Conn for her permission to publish her paper, "Hypericum, Herbs, and Health Policy."

Hypericum perforatum has been used for thousands of years by traditional healers as a botanical medicine. In Germany, hypericum is used to treat first and foremost, mild to moderate depression as well as anxiety and sleep disorder. In Germany, approximately three million prescriptions for hypericum are issued and almost 66 million daily doses of hypericum preparations are consumed annually.

Germany's Commission E is a special scientific committee of Bundesgesundheitsamt (Federal Department of Health), an independent division of the German Federal Health Agency. Since 1978 Commission E has actively engaged in collecting data on herbal medicines, evaluating their safety and efficacy and publishing the results in *Bundesanzeiger*, a publication similar to the *Federal Register*, in the form of brief monographs. Each monograph includes either a positive or negative assessment of whether a particular herb is safe and effective for over-the-counter use. The labeling of herbal products is based on the Commission's cautions and, when appropriate, an acknowledgment that a particular herb's efficacy may not be proven. Each monograph outlines the herb's action in the body, whether the medicinal (botanical) plant is free from side effects, the contraindications, as well as noting the proper schedule for its various dosage forms.

Commission E is comprised of a panel of experts specializing in the various aspects of medicinal plant research and use, including physicians, pharmacists, pharmacologists, toxicologists, representatives of the pharmaceutical industry, and consumers. The Commission requests studies from manufacturers in addition to information obtained from animal research, human clinical trials if available, epidemiological studies, historical usage information, clinical experience of physicians, and the subjective evaluations by patients. The panel of experts reviews the information and the Commission makes a judgment based on the results. The Commission's criteria for giving any herbal medicine its approval are that the herb must be absolutely proven to be safe and shown to be reasonably effective. Commission E's monograph lists *Hypericum perforatum* as an approved herb.

Commission E has published 312 monographs which cover 286 individual herbs and various herbal combinations. The German monographs have been recently translated into English and will be published by the American Botanical Council in the fall of 1996. The American Botanical Council is a nonprofit herb research and educational organization based in Austin, Texas. These monographs represent the most comprehensive and up-to-date herb information in the world.

In Canada, the Health Protection Branch convened an Expert Advisory Committee on Herbs and Botanical Preparations to study the labeling of herbal products in 1984. The Committee issued a report in 1986, recommending the establishment of a new class of remedies to be designated "Folklore Medicines." The Report of the Expert Advisory Committee on Herbs and Botanical Preparations sent to the Minister of National Health and Welfare led to significant developments by the Health Protection Branch. Regulatory procedures were established that permitted health claims to be made for herbs on the basis of information readily available in standard reference sources such as pharmacopeias, pharmacology books, or supportive references in general scientific and clinical literature. The Canadian regulatory system allows for the labeling of herbal medicines to inform the consumer regarding therapeutic uses of certain products as well as issuing regulations for proper dosage amounts.

The laws and regulations governing the sale and labeling of herbal medicines in the United States is the Food and Drug Administration (FDA), a division of the Department of Health and Human Services. The FDA is the federal agency that administers and enforces the Federal Food, Drug, and Cosmetic Act of 1938, (FFDCA) as amended. This Act provides the basis for the regulation of much of the testing, manufacture, distribution, and sale of food, drugs, cosmetics, and medical devices sold to the public. The FDA's social objective is to protect consumers health and well-being by preventing the dissemination of unsupported or insubstantial scientific information on food and dietary supplement labeling.

Extensive scientific research in the German-speaking countries has yielded a great deal of information on *Hypericum perforatum* and its effect on mild to moderate depression and anxiety. In comparison with other countries, the United States has done very little research on whole plant or crude plant extracts as medicinal agents. In the United States a plant cannot be patented. American pharmaceutical companies screen plants for biological activity and then the active compounds are isolated. If the active compounds are proven to be powerful enough, the drug companies will begin the process for a new drug application to procure FDA approval—an expensive and arduous process. Because of prohibitive costs and an absence of patent protection, very little incentive exists for the drug companies to actually engage in this arduous process.

In order to facilitate the use of vitamins, minerals, herbs, and botanicals to combat nutritional deficiencies and disease, portions of the FDCA, were amended by the *Dietary Supplement Health and Education Act of 1994* (DSHEA). The basic purpose of the DSHEA amendments to the FDCA is to ensure that the public has over-the-counter access to "dietary supplements," which include vitamins, minerals, amino acids, herbs and botanicals. In passing DSHEA, Congress made certain findings of fact related to the health of the American consumer, and specifically found that a rational federal regulatory framework was needed to supersede the current regulatory approach to dietary supplements. In order to accomplish this, DSHEA precludes the FDA from regulating "dietary supplements" as a "drug" solely because of any statements on the products labeling regarding claims that the product can treat or affect a nutritional deficiency or disease—unless the FDA determines that the product is not safe.

There is, however, still no formal way to evaluate health claims for herbs short of going through the new drug application process—a multimillion dollar commitment which is not cost effective for most herb companies. A rational federal regulatory system for the evaluation of therapeutic claims is not likely to materialize before the year 2000. DSHEA mandates that a seven-member committee of experts, appointed by the President, provide recommendations on how to evaluate health claims on supplement labels, including herbs. Under the provisions of DSHEA the panel will have two years to present its recommendations. The FDA will have another two years to formally draft the regulations. Presently, the labeling for dietary supplements must include only truthful, non-misleading, scientifically backed "statements of nutritional support" and "structure and function claims," which describe how a supplement alters the structure or function of the body.

It is hoped that in the FDA's efforts to understand medicinal herbs they will look to the efforts of other countries such as Germany's Commission E, and the Canadian regulatory system as a guide to drafting sensible regulation. Until such time, the American Botanical Council's English translation of the Commission E monographs can be used to empower consumers and also as a guide by pharmacists and health care professionals to help patients determine which herb should be taken for their specific health needs as well as address approved therapeutic uses, contraindications, safety data, dosage recommendations, and other pertinent information. Moreover, this could be used as a guide for the FDA in establishing labeling requirements for herbs in this country. Perhaps the United States might follow European policies that may make it more economically feasible for American companies and universities to research and develop herbs as medicines. Perhaps hypericum will lead the way.

Mary Elizabeth Conn, J.D., M.B.A.
P.O. Box 9005-502
La Mesa, California 91944
619-441-0339 (office)
619-441-7770 (fax)

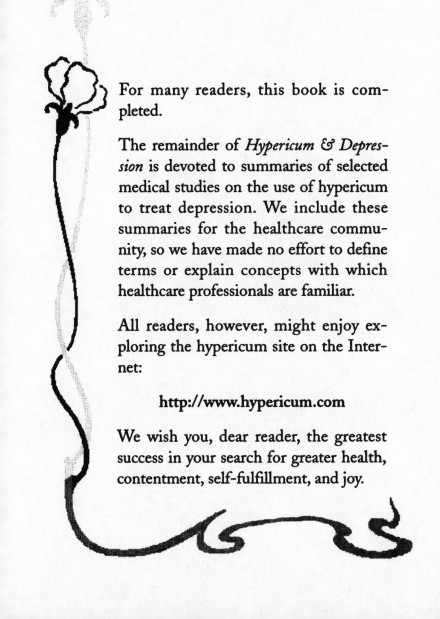

For many readers, this book is completed.

The remainder of *Hypericum & Depression* is devoted to summaries of selected medical studies on the use of hypericum to treat depression. We include these summaries for the healthcare community, so we have made no effort to define terms or explain concepts with which healthcare professionals are familiar.

All readers, however, might enjoy exploring the hypericum site on the Internet:

http://www.hypericum.com

We wish you, dear reader, the greatest success in your search for greater health, contentment, self-fulfillment, and joy.

Part Four

Medical Studies on
Hypericum and
Depression

Scientific Description of *Hypericum Perforatum*

Edited version of the ESCOP (European Scientific Corporation of Phytotherapy) Proposal of Product Characteristics

Definition

The drug St. John's wort consists of the dried above-ground part *of Hypericum perforatum L* collected shortly before or during the flowering period. It contains not less than 0.04% naphthodianthrones of the hypericin group (so-called total hypericin). Lower parts of the stem contain few active ingredients (2,3,4).

Components (4-21)

- Hypericum extracts contain at least ten components or groups of components that may contribute to the pharmacological effects. It is not yet possible to correlate the antidepressive mode of action with specific components; therefore, the pharmaceutical quality of the extracts was characterized on the basis of typical leading substances, especially the hypericins. The substances most involved in the antidepressant action are thought to be the hypericins and the flavonoids.

● The red-colored hypericins have been found in very few other plants while most of hypericum's other ingredients are common in the plant kingdom.

● The hypericins also have a photodynamic effect; sometimes they do not occur until the crude drug has been processed and exposed to light. The amount of total hypericin should be measured after light exposition, which transforms the biological precursors, protohypericin and protopseudo-hypericin, into hypericin and pseudohypericin (5-8).

● The concentration of hypericins (mainly hypericin and pseudohypericin) in buds and flowers can vary between 0.06% and 0.75%. The usual concentration is 0.1-0.15%, but lower concentrations (less than 0.1%) might result from harvesting of lower parts of the herb (4). A minimum content of 0.04% total hypericin is required for commercial use.

● Other possible active ingredients are polymerization products of hypericin, the flavonoids quercetin, hyperoside, quercitrin, isoquercitrin, rutin, campherol, luteolin, and 13-118-biapigenin, the total concentration of which can amount to 2% to 4%.

● The 1,3,6,7-tetra-hydroxyxanthone, the aglycone of the mangiferin found in other species of *Hypericum*, is only present in concentrations of 0.0004%.

● The procyanidines, which are related to the flavonoids, account for about 8%.

● Hyperforin, with a structure related to the hop bitters humulon and lupulon, contributes to about 2.8%.

Pharmaceutical form

Hypericum is available in tablets, capsules, drops and teas. It is also available as an oil for external use.

The oil cannot be recommended for internal use as an antidepressant.

Therapeutic indications

The official German commission monograph lists mild to moderate depressive states (22-51), fear, and nervous disturbances, and somatoform disturbances as clinical indications for hypericum.

Most of the scientific documentation on hypericum has been performed on mild to moderate depressions. Treatment of severe depressions (with suicidal, psychotic or severe melancholic features) with hypericum preparations is not yet recommended.

Clinical effect (22-51,109-110)

Besides numerous case reports and drug monitoring studies (with more than 5,000 patients) on the efficacy and safety of standardized St. John's wort preparations, 25 controlled double-blind studies (with more than 2,000 patients) have been conducted. The major indication was mild to moderate depressive disorders.

Sixteen of the studies compared hypericum with placebo (sugar-pills) and 9 with reference treatments (Imipramine-2 (34, 44), Amitryptilin-2 (32, 48), Maprotiline-1 (46), Desipramine-1(30), Diazepam-2 (27,29), and Light-therapy (47).

In most of the studies, both depressive symptoms (depressed mood, anxiety, loss of interest, feelings of worthlessness, decreased activity) and secondary symptoms (sleep disturbance, lack of concentration, somatic complaints) improved significantly (see Figure 1) (25).

Fig. 1. Severity of symptoms before and after treatment with Hypericum for 4 weeks in 3250 patients measured by GCI

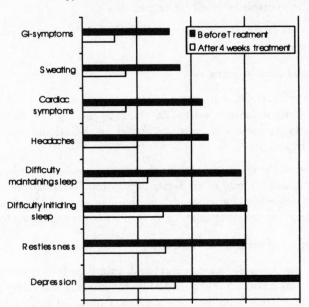

Results are summarized in Table 1. Some facts:

● The response rate has generally been between 50 and 80%, comparable to that of low- to medium dose treatment with "classic" synthetic antidepressants.

● In three of the trials (39,45,109) there waswere no statistically significant difference between hypericum and placebo. In a criteria-based clinical review by Ernst (110) two of these studies also were judged as questionable because of methodological weaknesses. The third one is a yet unpublished study. They were all made with low dose hypericum test medications.

● Hypericum leads to an increase in deep sleep and does not impair cognitive functions or the ability to work or drive a car (83, 85).

● Hypericum has been shown to have a long-term effect on anxiety comparable to Bromazepam and Diazepam (29, 35).

● A Russian study (102) showed good results combining hypericum with psychotherapy to treat alcoholics with peptic ulcers.

● A preliminary study by Martinez et al. also showed an effect comparable to light therapy in the treatment of seasonal affective disorder (47).

● Antiinflammatory and antibacterial effects of externally applied St. John's wort preparations have been reported and attributed to the presence of hyperforin. (1).

Hypericin has also been proven to possess promising anticancer properties and has been shown to inhibit growth of gliomas (brain tumors) (103), lung cancer (104) and skin cancer (68) in vitro (in the laboratory). Its photodynamic properties might lead to the use of hypericin in combination with lasers in the photodynamic treatment of cancer (68).

Table 1

Summary of 25 randomized clinical studies and two drug-monitoring studies on the efficiency of Hypericum in the treatment of depression and anxiety.

Authors year	No of cases	Total hypericin/day	We-eks	Target Parameters	Test preparation	Respons rate	Compared treatment	Resp. rate	rat-ing
Witte, 1995	97	0.5 mg x2	6	HAMD, D-S	Psychotonin	79 %	Placebo	56%	-
Ditzler, 1994	60	0.24 mg x2	8	D-S	Neurapas***	67%	Placebo	33%	-
Albrecht, 1994	1060	0.3 mg x3	4	HAMD, D-S	Jarsin	75%	None	-	-
Woelk, 1993	3250	0.9 mg x3	4	D-S	Jarsin 300	82%	None	-	-
Sommer, 1993	105	0.9 mg x3	4	HAMD	Jarsin 300	67%	Placebo	28%	41
Huebner, 1993	40	0.9 mg x3	4	HAMD, B-L.CGI	Jarsin 300	70%	Placebo	47%	54
Hänsgen, 1993	100	0.9 mg x3	6	HAMD, D-S, CGI, BEB	Jarsin 300	81%	Placebo	26%	55
Vorbach, 1993	135	0.9 mg x3	6	HAMD, D-S, CGI	Jarsin 300	82%	Imipramin	62%	74
Harrer, 1993	102	1 mg x 3	4	HAMD, D-S, CGI	Jarsin 300	61%	Maprotilin,	67%	70
Bergmann, 1993	76	0.25mg x3	6	HAMD, Bf-S	Esbericum	84%	Amitrypilin	74%	38
Martinez, 1993	20	0.9 mg x3	4	HAMD, (SAD-patients)	Jarsin + 300 Lux	60%	Jarsin + 3000Lux	72%	38
König, 1993	112	0.5-1mg x 2	6	Bf-S	Extract Z 90017	53%	Placebo	53%	-
Lehrl, 1993	50	0.37 mg x 3	4	HAMD, KAI	Jarsin	42%	Placebo	25%	25
Schmidt, 1993	65	0.37 mg x 3	6	HAMD, Cognition	Jarsin	67%	Placebo	26.7%	-

Study	n	Dose	Weeks	Scales	Medication	Response	Comparator	Response	
Quandt, 1993	88	0,37 mg x 3	4	HAMD	Psychotonin M	70,7%	Placebo	7,7%	49
Reh, 1992	50	0,5mg x 2	8	HAMD	Neuroplant	70%	Placebo	45%	55
Ostercheider, 1992	46	0,25mg x2	8	HAMD	Neuroplant	0%	Placebo	0%	25
Harrer, 1991	116	0,37 mg x 3	6	HAMD, HAMA, D-S	Psychotonin	75%	Placebo	25%	52
Halama, 1991	50	0,3 mg x 3	4	HAMD, B-L, CGI	Jarsin	60%	Placebo	12%	55
Werth, 1989	30	0,37 mg x 3	3,5	HAMD after amputation	Psychotonin M	73%	Imipramin	60%	43
Schmidt, 1989	40	0,37 mg x 3	4	HAMD , STAI	Psychotonin M	65%	Placebo	33%	-
Knuebel, 1988	130	0,1 mg x 2*	6	HAMD, CGI, Bf-S	Sedariston	88%	Amitryptilin	80%	35
Schilch, 1987	49	0,25 mg x 3	4	HAMD	Psychotonin M	28,4%	Placebo	-23%	45
Warnecke, 1986	60	0,3mg x 2	12	HAMA, SDS, CGI	Hyperforat	77%**	Diazepam	50%	-
Steger, 1985	93	0,1 mg x2 *	6	CGI, D-S, B-L	Sedariston	70%	Desipramin	30%	-
Panijel, 1985	100	0,1 mg x2*	2	CGI, B-L, STAI	Sedariston	78%**	Diazepam	54%	-
Hoffmann, 1979	60	3 mg x 3	6	Own Scale	Hyperforat	61.4%	Placebo	15.2%	16

D-S = Depression Scale according to von Zerssen; CGI = Clinical Global Impression score; B–L = von Zerssen Health Compliant survey; BEB = Hänsgens complaint inventory; Bf-S = v. Zerssen's SelfRating Scale; STAI = State Trait Anxiety Inventory ; KAI = Lehrl's Short Test on General Information processing;

SAD = Seasonal Affective Disorders, SDS =Self Rating Depression Scale * = + 50 mg Valeriana in combination-medication. ** Measured by CGI

*** combination medication with Hypericum, Valeria, Passiflorae, Coridalis cavae and Eschscholixiae californiae

Dosage

There is much confusion in the literature about how to specify the exact dosage of hypericum. The most common way is in mg of total extract. As the strengths of the extracts differ considerably, we have chosen to use mg of total hypericin, which means the dose of all the different hypericins (hypericin, pseudohypericin, protopseudohypericin, etc.) together. One way to get the correct dosage is to multiply the dose in mg times the percentage of total hypericin.

ESCOP recommendation is 0.2-1.0 mg total hypericin daily (1).

This recommendation is a bit low in our opinion, as most of the research shows a trend towards better results with higher doses (70, 105).

The preceding table shows that the mean response rate with Jarsin 300 (= 2.7 mg standard hypericin daily) is 70% and with the other preparations 60%. This is not a very scientific method of finding the proper dose, but better than nothing while we wait for further studies on this subject.

The findings by Perovic et al. of an almost linear dose-response serotonin reuptake inhibitory effect also point in this direction.

Winterhoff et al. (70) have demonstrated in animal experiments that 125 mg hypericum extract LI 160 (= 0.35 mg total hypericin) has an equal effect to 10 mg Imipramine on rats. For good clinical results we therefore recommend 0.9 mg total hypericin three times daily (= equivalent to 75 mg Imipramine).

For those who have very mild symptoms or felt some kind of side-effects on the high-dose treatment, the dose can be lowered to 2-3x 0.25-0.35 mg daily.

For children aged 6-12 we recommend treatment with half the adult dose (1).

It is recommended to take hypericum with food in order to minimize possible gastrointestinal complaints.

No studies have been performed on the effect of hypericum teas. 10-20% of total hypericin gets dissolved into tea at a temperature of 80° C (62). For tea-infusion the ESCOP recommends 2-4 g of dried herb daily. However, if the mean concentration in the plant's upper parts is 0.1%, and 10-20% dissolves into the tea, it means that you have to take 10-20g of fresh leaves to get 2 mg of total hypericin.

As alcohol is a better solvent (approximately 35% gets dissolved at a temperature of 80° C), a schnapps made with 6g of fresh hypericum buds would be enough to get 2 mg of total hypericin (62).

Duration of treatment

The ESCOP does not set any restrictions concerning duration of treatment. The effect of hypericum seems to be very long-term. If the response rate is 60% after four weeks, it is likely to be 70% after six weeks and 80% after eight weeks. (See Figure 2).

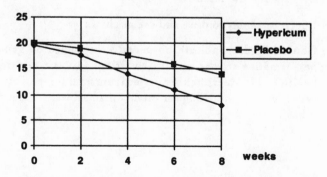

Figure 2 HAMD development in the study by Reh et al 1992.

Interactions

The ESCOP does not mention any known interactions and there are no known severe interactions reported from millions of treatments. As recent research has demonstrated a SRI effect, we recommend special monitoring and care when combined with other antidepressants, especially MAO-inhibitors, because of the theoretical risk of creating a serotonin syndrome. Some manufacturers also mention possible risk of photosensitivity when hypericum is used together with other photosensitizing drugs such as Chlorpromazine and Tetracyclines. There is no interaction with alcohol (112). The lack of interactions is a great advantage, especially in the treatment of the elderly, who often take many other medications with many possibilities of adverse interactions.

Pregnancy and lactation

No data available. As Winterhoff et al. have demonstrated that hypericum extract inhibits the pituitary secretion of prolactin (70), there might be a theoretical possibility of problems with the production of breast-milk during lactation. If this happens one can simply lower the dose or stop taking hypericum. Besides being a hormone necessary for the production of breast-milk, prolactin also has an inhibiting effect on the menstrual cycle and on the libido (sex drive). A lowering of the prolactin does not pose any risk for the infant.

Effects on ability to drive and use machines

Clinical studies indicate no negative influence on general performance or the ability to drive. On the contrary, healthy volunteers taking hypericum extract performed better in tests simulating car driving than subjects taking placebos (83).

Undesirable effects

None confirmed at dose levels up to 3 mg total hypericin. Photosensitization might occur at much higher dosages (see Overdose). Some manufacturers warn of photosensitization when hypericum is used in high doses by light-skinned persons who stay out in the sun a lot.

In a drug-monitoring study with 3,250 patients on high-dose hypericum treatment (0.9 mg x 3) 0.4% of the patients had allergic reactions (skin rash) (25). About 2% complained of gastrointestinal problems, tiredness and other problems that also could have been secondary to their depression (25). In another drug-monitoring study of 1,040 patients (26) on a lower dose (0.36 mg x 3), there were no complaints whatsoever of adverse skin reactions (26).

In placebo-controlled studies there has never been any difference in amount of side effects between the placebo and trial groups. On the contrary, the placebo group sometimes had more side effects, possibly due to untreated depression (40). In a summary of 15 placebo controlled studies performed on 1008 patients there was no difference concerning amount of side-effects (4.1% on hypericum and 4.8% on placebo), and actually less treatment dropouts because of side effects among patients treated with hypericum (0.4% versus 1,6%) (111).

Overdose

Photosensitization at high dosage is reported during experimental antiviral treatment with synthetic hypericin (35 mg intravenously) in HIV-infected patients. Typical phytotoxic symptoms include an itching rash and blisters of the skin 24 hours after exposure to sunlight (58). The symptoms are generally mild and do not create any long-term damage.

Inflammatory reactions in the gastrointestinal tract, pain and vomiting may result from an overdose due to catechine-type tannins (1).

Treatment consists of avoiding light exposure, emptying of the stomach, lavage with protein-containing liquids (gruel, protein broth) milk if need be.

Contraindications

None known.

Pharmacodynamic properties

Numerous clinical studies have shown that hypericum possesses an antidepressant effect of a magnitude similar to synthetic antidepressants, but with a minimum of side effects.

The pharmacological mechanism, though, is still a matter of debate. There are many hypotheses, and it seems likely that hypericum uses many different modes of action simultaneously. Maybe one can see the antidepressant effect of hypericum as an example of the old proverb, "Many small streams together create a great river."

Tissue distribution

One interesting notion is that hypericin is absorbed very slowly, and excreted even more slowly in the brain, skin and stomach of mice. This means there will be a gradual increase of concentration in these tissues over a period of weeks until a steady state is reached (68).

This might explain its slow mode of action, its benign effect-side-effect profile and why its primary sites of action have been in the brain, skin and GI-system. These organs are also the organs considered to be primarily affected by hypericum in traditional medicine (see Figure 3). Hypericin gradually accumulates in these tissues over time, while it passes through other parts of the body rapidly.

Figure 3

Hypericin retention in % after 7 days compared to peak uptake

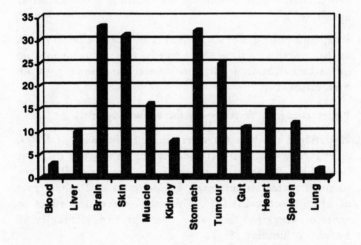

Serotonin and norepinephrine reuptake inhibitory effect

In a recent study Perovic et al. have demonstrated a seroto-nin-reuptake-inhibiting effect of hypericum extract in vitro (69). (Low serotonin levels in the synapses between the nerve cells are believed to be one of the primary causes of clinical depression. Inhibiting the reuptake of serotonin in the nerve cells raises the concentration of serotonin.) Müller et al. have demonstrated that hypericum also inhibits norepinephrine uptake (67).

It remains to be established whether this has a clinical effect, as the concentrations of the active ingredients of hypericum in the human brain during antidepressive treatment have not been established.

Effect on cortisol secretion via the immune system

Hypericum inhibits the stress-induced increase of CRH, ACTH and cortisol-secretion by inhibiting the cytokine interleukin-6 and other cytokines excreted by cells of the immune system (monocytes, lymphocytes and other types of white blood cells) (71). This stress-preventing effect on cortisol secretion has also been proven clinically in healthy volunteers (59,70).

(It has been proven that depression causes an increased secretion of the "stress hormones" CRH, ACTH and cor-tisol. These hormones also have a inhibitory effect on the immune system as well as lots of other effects that could explain some of the physiological changes in depression. The cytokines excreted by white blood cells can also be part of these effects both on their own and by their effect on the cortisol secretion).

MAO-inhibition insufficient

The MAO-inhibitory effect of hypericum demonstrated by Suzuki et al. (108) has not been confirmed in later investigations in an amount sufficient to explain the antidepressant action, although it could still be one of the small streams that create the river (61,62). (MAO, mono-amino-oxidase, is an enzyme that contributes to the breakdown of the neurotransmitters serotonin and norepinephrine. An inhibition of MAO thus results in an inhibition of the breakdown, which results in an increase of neurotransmitters in the synapses).

Effect on melatonin secretion

In a study with 13 healthy volunteers, increased light-induced suppression of melatonin and a significant increase in the nocturnal melatonin plasma concentration was observed after administration of hypericum for three weeks. This effect on the melatonin secretion has also been observed with synthetic antidepressants like Amitryptilin and Desipamin (86).

(Melatonin is a hormone excreted by the pineal gland; it has great importance for the regulation of biological rhythms, sleep and sexual activity. The excretion is inhibited by light and facilitated by darkness. Some disturbances in biological rhythms, sexual activity and sleep during depression could be due to detrimental effects on the melatonin system.)

Increased secretion of urinary neurotransmitter metabolites after administration of hypericum

A significant increase of urinary neurotransmitter metabolites of serotonin and norepinephrine has been observed after treatment with hypericum (82). This indicates that hypericum, like other antidepressants, might increase the concentration of these neurotransmitters in the brain.

Effect on dopamine and prolactin metabolism

Hypericum inhibits the enzyme dopamine-B-hydroxylase in vitro (64). (Dopamine-B-hydroxylase breaks down the neurotransmitter dopamine, which is involved in the patophysiology of schizophrenic psychosis and Parkinson's disease.) The resulting increase of dopamine increases the production of a prolactin-inhibitory factor, which in turn diminishes the secretion of Prolactin (70). (Prolactin is a hormone necessary for the production of breast-milk. It also has an inhibiting effect on the menstrual cycle and on the libido.)

Effect on benzodiazepine receptors

Hypericin has been shown to potentiate binding to benzodiazepine receptors. This could be one explanation for hypericum's antianxiety effects (65). (Benzodiazepine receptors are involved in the antianxiety and tranquilizing effect of Valium, Rohypnol and other preparations of the benzodiazepine group)

Nice mice

Animal studies in mice treated with hypericum have revealed CNS activities which can be interpreted as an antidepressant effect. Aggressive behavior was significantly reduced and physical activity was enhanced (72).

Typical sedative effects on the ethanol-induced sleeping time in mice have also been demonstrated.

In the so-called forced-swimming or Porsolt test hypericum showed an effect on mice equal to Imipramine (70).

Reserpine antagonism

Oral administration of hypericin in mice resulted in a reserpine antagonism, which is also indicative of antidepressant effects (72).

Effects on EEG, sleep EEG and evoked potentials

The effect of hypericum extract was tested on the electroencephalogram (EEG) of 40 depressive patients after 4 weeks of treatment (34). The results have been interpreted as predominantly relaxing effects (increase in theta activity, decrease in alpha activity and no change in beta activity). Compared to the decrease of alertness after Bromazepam (a sedative of the benzodiazepine group), this particular effect on alpha waves was much smaller after administration of St. John's wort.

In another EEG study a reduction in the alpha and an increase in the theta and beta frequencies as well as a diminished latency in visual and acoustically evoked potentials was shown. Four weeks' treatment resulted in an increase of deep-sleep phases (83).

In a study with 24 healthy volunteers the effects of hypericum on the resting EEG as well as on visually and acoustically evoked potentials were compared with Maprotiline (a synthetic AD). In resting EEG the medications had opposite effects on the theta frequencies (increase with St. John's wort and decrease with Maprotiline) and mainly similar changes in alpha and beta frequencies. The overall results of the study have been interpreted as a tendency of improved of perception and clarity of mind due to treatment with hypericum (85).

(EEG [electroencephalogram] measures the electric activity of the brain by means of electrodes placed in certain positions. The brain waves are described as follows: 13-26 cycles per second (cps) is beta, 8-12 cps is alpha, 6-8 is theta, and 3-5 is delta. The beta waves are most prominent when you are awake and doing focused activities, the alpha waves in relaxation with eyes closed, and the delta waves in deep sleep. The theta waves occur during sleep as well but have also been associated with deep meditation, serene pleasure and heightened creativity. Visually and acoustically evoked potentials are a way to measure the alertness and reaction time of the nervous system.)

Pharmacokinetics

In two investigations the bio-availability of hypericin and pseudohypericin was studied in 12 volunteers (89, 90).

● The median maximal plasma levels were 1.5, 4.1, and 14.2 ng/ml for hypericin and 2.7, 11.7, and 30.6 ng/ml for pseudohypericin, respectively, for the three doses given above (interim evaluation of four volunteers).

● The median elimination half-life times of hypericin were 24.8 to 26.5 hours, and varied for pseudohypericin from 16.3 to 36.0 hours.

● Ranging between 2.0 to 2.6 hours, the median lag-time of absorption was remarkably prolonged for hypericin when compared to pseudohypericin (0.3 to 1.1 hours).

● The areas under the curves (AUC) showed a nonlinear increase with raising dose; this effect was statistically significant for hypericin.

● During long-term dosing (3 x 300 mg/day), a steady state was reached after 4 days.

● Mean maximal plasma level during the steady-state treatment was 8.5 ng/ml for hypericin and 5.8 ng/ml for pseudohypericin, while mean trough levels were 5.3 ng/ml for hypericin and 3.7 ng/ml for pseudohypericin.

● In spite of their structural similarities, there are substantial pharmacokinetic differences between hypericin and pseudohypericin.

Preclinical safety data

Acute administration

No data available.

Subchronic administration

Not relevant.

Note: Photosensitization caused by St. John's wort is mainly known from veterinary studies (91,94). Phytotoxic symptoms occurred in a dose-dependent manner in light-colored cattle after substantial feeding on fresh St. John's wort. From this finding it is estimated that a 30-fold therapeutic dose might cause phytotoxic symptoms in humans. In a study with the IV application of synthetic hypericin in HIV-infected patients, reversible symptoms of phytotoxicity were observed at the highest dosage scheme, which was 35 times higher than the highest oral dosage of total hypericin used in the therapy of depressive disorders (2). In therapeutic relevant concentrations of total hypericin in depressive disorders, i.e., up to 1 mg daily over 30 days, it was shown in an experimental, double-blind placebo-controlled study with 40 volunteers that no photosensitivity was induced (57).

Mutagenicity

Not relevant.

References:

1. ESCOP Proposal for the Summary of Product Characteristics 3rd version May 1994.

2. Deutscher Arzneimittel-Codex, (German drug-codex, DAC 1986), 3. Erg. 91. Monographie Johanniskraut.

3. Pharmacopée Francaise (French drug codex), X ed. 1994. Monogaph Millepertuis.

4. Hänsel R, Keller K, Rimpler H, Schneider G, eds. :Hagers Handbuch der Pharmazeutischen Praxis, Band 5: Drogen E-O.

5. Brockmann H, Haschad MN, Maier K, Pohl F. :Naturwissenschaften 1939;27:550

6. Brockmann H, Franssen V, Spitzner D, Augustiniak H. :Tetrahedron Lett 1974: 1991-94

7. Schütt H, Hölzl J. :Pharmazie 1994; 49:206-9

8. Krämer W, Wiartalla R. :Pharm Ztg Wiss 1992;5 202-7

9. Häberlein H, Tschiersch KP, Stock S, Hölzl J. :Pharm Ztg Wiss 1992;4: 169-74

10. Berghöfer R. :Marburg Dissertation 1987.

11. Sektion Medizin des Osteuropa-Institutes der Freien Universität Berln, eds Arzneipflanzen in der Sowjetunion, :Reihe Medizin, Heft 44, 1966:134,135.

12. Hölzl J, Ostrowsky E. :Dtsch Apoth Ztg 1987;127:1227-30

13. Stock S. :Marburg Dissertation 1987

14. Berghöfer R, Hölzl J. Planta Med 1987; 53216,217

15. Berghöfer R, Hölzl J. Planta Med 1987;

16. Roth L. :Hypericum, Hypericin, Botanik, Inhaltstoffe, Wirkung. : Landsberg: ecomed Verlagsgesellschaft mbH 1990:28-87, 97-121.

17. Sparenberg D. :Marburg Dissertation 1993.

18. Maizenbacher P. :Tübingen: Dissertation 1991.

19. Melzer R, Fricke U, Hölzl J. Arzneim Forsch 1991;41:481-3.

20. Maisenbacher P, Kovar KA. : Planta Med 1992;58:291-3

21 .Ostrowsky E. :Marburg Dissertation 1988

22. Daniel K. Klin Wschr 1951;29:260-2.

23. Pieschl D, Angersbach P, Toman P. :Therapiewoche 1989;39:2567-71

24. Meisenbacher IU, Kuhn U. :Natura Med 1990;7:394-9.

25. Woelk H, Burkard G, Grünvald J. :Nervenheilkunde 1993;12:308-13: translated to J Geriatr Psychiatry Neurol 1994; 7(suppl 1): S34-38

26. Albecht W, Hübner W-D, Podzuweit H, Schmidt U, : Der Kassenarzt, Heft 41, 1994, 45-54.

27. Warnecke G. : Z Allg Med 1986;62:1111-13

28. Hoffman J, Kühl ED. :Z Allg Med 1979;776-82

29. Panijel M, :Therapiwoche 1985 41:4659-4668

30. Steger W. : Z Allg Med 1985; 61: 914-18

31. Schlich D, Braukmann, Schenk N. :Psycho 1987; 13:440-7.

32. Kniebel R, Burchard JM. : Z Allg Med 1988, 64, 689-696

33. Schmidt D, Schenk N, Schwarz I, Vorberg G. :Psycho 1989; 15:665-71.

34. Werth W. Der Kassenarzt 1989; 15:64-68

35. Kugler J. Weidenhammer W, Scmidt A, Groll S. : Z Allg Med 1990; 66:21-29

36. Halama P. Nervenhilkunde 1991; 10:250-253

37. Harrer G, Schmidt U, Kuhn U. : TW Neurol Psychiatr 1991; 5:710-716

38. Reh C, Laux P, Schenk N. :Therapiewoche 1992; 42:1576-81

39. Osterheider M, Schmidtke A, Beckmann H. Fortchr Neurol. Psychiatr 1992;60. Sonderheft 2:210-211

40. Harrer G, Sommer H. Münch med Wschr 1993;135:305-9

41. Hübner W-D, Lande S, Podzuweit H :Nervenheilkunde 1993, 12:278-280, translated to J Geriatr Psychiatry Neurol 1994; 7(suppl 1): S12-14

42. Hänsgen KD, Vesper J, Ploch M. :Nervenheilkunde 1993, 12:285-9, translated to J Geriatr Psychiatry Neurol 1994; 7(suppl 1): S15-18

43. Quandt J, Schmidt U, Schenk N. : Allgemeinarzt 1993;15:97-102

44. Vorbach EU, Hübner WD, Arnoldt KH. :Nervenheilkunde 1993, 12:290-96, translated to J Geriatr Psychiatry Neurol 1994; 7(suppl 1): S19-23.

45. Lehrl S, Woelk H :Nervenheilkunde 1993, 12:281-84

46. Harrer G, Hübner WD, Podzuweit H, :Nervenheilkunde 1993, 12:297-301, translated to J Geriatr Psychiatry Neurol 1994; 7(suppl 1): S24-28

47. Martinez B, Kasper S, Ruhrmann B, Möller HJ. :Nervenheilkunde 1993, 12:302-7, translated to J Geriatr Psychiatry Neurol 1994; 7(suppl 1): S29-33

48. Bergmann R, Nüssner J, Demling J. TW Neurol Psychiatr 1993;19:339-42

49. Schmidt U, Sommer H. Fortschr Med 1993;19:339-42

50. Witte-B; Harrer-G; Kaptan-T; Podzuweit-H; Schmidt-U. :Fortschr-Med. 1995 Oct 10; 113(28): 404-8

51. Pahlow M. :Dtsch Apoth Zt 1984;124:2059-60

52. Hölzl J. Therapeutikon 1989;3:540-7

53. Hobbs C. Herbal Gram 1989:24-33

54. Herberg KW. Therapiewoche 1994;44:xxx

55. Siegers CP; Biel S, Wilhelm KP. Nervenheilkunde 1993, 12:320-322

56. Hölzl J, Stock S. :Med Mo Pharm 1991;14:304-6

57. Wienert V, Classen R, Hiller KO. :Lübeck-Travemünde 1991, 3. Phytotherapie-Kongress:Poster P23.

58. James JS. :AIDS Treatment News 1992;146:1-4

59. Demisch L. Hölzl J. Pharm Ztg Wiss 1993;6:50-4.

60. Sparenberg B, Demisch L, Hölzl J. Pharm Ztg Wiss 1993;6:50-4

61. Thiede HM, Walper A. Nervenheilkunde 1993;12: translated to J Geriatr Psychiatry Neurol 1994; 7(suppl 1): 54-56.

62. Bladt S, Wagner H. :Nervenheilkunde 1993, 12:346-348, translated to J Geriatr Psychiatry Neurol 1994; 7(suppl 1): S57-59

63. Curle P, Kato G, Hiller KO, Battelle-Report

64. Nielsen M, Froekjaer S, Braestrup C. Biochem Pharmacol 1988;37:3285-7

65. Obry, M München Dissertation 1991.

66. Müller WEG, Rossol R. :Nervenheilkunde 1993, 12:357-8, translated to J. Geriatr. Psychiatry Neurol 1994; 7(suppl 1): S63-64.

67. Müller WEG, Schäfer C :Dtsch Apotheker Zeitung 1996 136: 13 1015-1022

68. Chung-PS; Saxton-RE; Paiva-MB; Rhee-CK; Soudant-J; Mathey-A; Foote-C; Castro-DJ : Laryngoscope. 1994 Dec; 104(12): 1471-6

69. Perovic-S and Mueller-W-E-G :Arzneimittel-Forschung/Drug Research 45(II), 11, 1145-1148(1995)

70. Winterhoff H, Butterweck V, Nahrstedt A, Gumbinger H.G, Schulz V, Erping S, Bosshammer F, Wieligman A, :"Phytopharmaka in Forschung unf klinischer Anwendung"

Loew D :1995 Steinkopff Verlag GmbH & Co. KG. Darmstadt
S39-52

71. Thiele B, Brink I, Ploch M. :Nervenheilkunde 1993, 12:353-6,
translated to J. Geriatr. Psychiatry Neurol 1994 7(suppl1): S60-62.

72. Okpanyi SN, Weischer ML. : Arzneim Forsch Drug Res
1987:37:10-3

73.Anderson DO, Weber ND, Wood SG, Hughes BG, Murray
BK, North JA. Antiviral Res 1991;16:185-96.

74. Barnard DL, Huffman JH, Moris JLB, Wood SG, Hughes
BG, Sidwell RW, :Antiviral Res 1992;17:63-77

75. Hudson JB, Lopez-Bazzocchi I, Towers GHN. :Antiviral Res
1991;15:101-12.

76. Hudson JB, Harris L, Towers GHN. :Antiviral Res 1993; 20-
:173-8.

77. Kraus GA, Pratt D, ossberg J, Carpenter S. Biochem Piophys
Res Commun 1990;172:149-53.

78. Lavie G, Valentin F, Levin B, Mazur Y, Gallo G, Lavie D,
Weiner D, Meruelo D. :Proc Natl Acad Sci 1989;86:5693-8.

79. Meruelo D. Lavie G, Lavie D, :Proc Natl Acad Sci 1988;
85:5230-4.

80. Schinazi RF, Chu CK, Babu JR, Oswald BJ,

81. Takahashi J, Nakanishi S, Kobayashi E, Nakano H, Suzuki K,
Tamaoki T. Biochem Biophys Res Commun 1989, 165:1207-12.

82. Müldner H, Zöller M. Arzneim Forsch 1984;34:918-20.

83. Johnson D. Nervenheilkunde 1991;10:316-7

84. Schulz H, Jobert M. Nervenheilkunde 1993; 12:323-7.

85. Johnson D, Ksciuk H, Woelk H, Sauerwein-Giese E, Frauendorf
A. :Nervenheilkunde 1993, 12:328-30, translated to J. Geriatr. Psychiatry Neurol 1994; 7(suppl 1): S44-46

86. Demisch L. Sielaff T, Nispel J, Gebhart P, Köhler C, Pflug B,
:Nürnberg 191: AGNP-symposium Abstract.

87. Brondz I, Greirokk T, Groth PA, Aasen AJ. Tetrahedron Lett
1982;23:1299-1300.

88. Stock S, Hölzl J. Planta Med 1991;57 (Suppl2):A61-2.Geriatr.
Psychiatry Neurol 1994; 7(suppl 1): S47-53.

91. Araya OS, Ford EJH, J Comp Pathol Soc 1941; 63:2570-4

92. Giese AC. Photochem Photobiol 1980; 5:229-55

93. Pace N, MacKinney G. J Am Chem Soc 1941; 63:2570-4

94. Pace N. :Am J Physiol 1942;136:650-6.

95. Knudsen I., ed :Genetic Toxicologiy of the Diet. New York: Alan R Liss, 1986:33-43

96. U.S. Department of Health and Human services, ed Research Triangle Park 1991: NTH Publication No. 91-3140.

97. Ito N. Japanese J Cancer Res 1992;83:312-3

98. Hirono I. Japanese J Cancer Res 1992;83:313-4

99. Bootman I. LSR-Report No 87/SIR 008/647, unpublished.

100. Okpanyi SN, Lidzba H, Scholl BC, Miltenburger HG. :Arzneim Forsch 1990;40:851-4.

101 Ernst E :Fortschritte der Medizin 1995 Sep 10;113(25):354-5

102.Krylov-AA; Ibatov-A :Vrach-Delo. 1993 Feb-Mar(2-3): 146-8

103. Couldwell-WT; Gopalakrishna-R; Hinton-DR; He-S; Weiss-MH; Law-RE; Apuzzo-ML :Neurosurgery. 1994 Oct; 35(4): 705-9; discussion 709-10

104. Gopalakrishna-R; Chen-ZH; Gundimeda-U. :SO: Proc-Natl-Acad-Sci-U-S-A. 1994 Dec 6; 91(25): 12233-7

105. Jarsin 300 Product Information Lichtwer Pharma GmbH, Berlin, Germany.

106. Lavie-G, Mazur-Y, Lavie-D, Meruelo-D : Medicinal Research Reviews, Vol 15 No. 2, 111-119 (1995)

107. Linden-M; Osterheider-M; Schaaf-B; et al. Munch Med Wschr 1992; 134: 836-840.

108. Suzuki O, Katsumata Y, Chari M, :Plant med 1984, 42.17-23

109. König-CD, University of Basel 1993 (Thesis)

110. Ditzler-B, Gessner-B, Schatton-W, Willems-M :Complementary Therapies in medicine, 1994; 7(suppl):24-8

111. Linde-K, Ramirez-G, Murow-C, Pauls-A, Weidenhammer-W, Melchart-D: BMJ 1996; 313:253-8

112 Schmidt-U, Harrer-G, Kuhn-U : Nervenheilkunde 1993; 12:314-319.

Studies Comparing Hypericum with Synthetic Drugs

Summary and general comments

● There are at least eight randomized, double-blind studies comparing the antidepressant and anxiolytic effect of *Hypericum perforatum* to reference medications. The reference substances were Imipramine (2 studies), Amitryptilin (2 studies), Diazepam (2 studies) Maprotiline, and Desipramine . There is also one study comparing hypericum and Maprotiline regarding their effect on EEG and evoked potentials in healthy volunteers that will be referred in another section.

● Two of the studies against Desipramine and diazepam were conducted with a combination preparation of hypericum and Valeria.

● Generally one has found a comparable antidepressant and anxiolytic effect of hypericin to low-to medium dose treatment with synthetic antidepressants, and a more benign side-effect profile. It is interesting to note that side effects generally are more common when hypericum is compared to reference substances than when it is compared to a placebo.

● In many of the placebo-controlled studies the amount of "side effects" and dropouts because of adverse drug reactions were more frequent in the placebo than in the hypericum groups! This clearly demonstrates the vast importance of suggestions and expectations for treatment results with moderately to mildly depressed patients. It also clearly demonstrates the difficulties in deciding whether physical complaints during treatment are due to side effects or are secondary to the depression.

● It has also been demonstrated that the role of placebo and suggestions decreases with severity of depression.

● Hypericum proved superior to Imipramine in a moderate dose on severe depressions (HAMD->21) in the study by Vorbach et al. This contradicts the findings of other researchers, who only recommend hypericum for the treatment of mild to moderate depressions. More studies are needed to further investigate this.

● It is also interesting to note the long-range effects of hypericum. It seems obvious that the effect continues to accumulate over a long time so that studies conducted over a longer period of time (6 weeks) generally show more significant effects. More studies that follow hypericum treatment for a longer period of time are needed in order to investigate the true therapeutic opportunities.

● All the researchers involved clearly recommend hypericum for the treatment of mild to moderate depressions in outpatient clinics due to its broad therapeutic window, benign effect-side-effect profile and good compliance.

● In this book we will take a further look at four of these studies.

● The results of the studies are summarized in Table 2.

Study 1

Effectiveness and tolerance of the hypericum extract LI 160 in comparison with Imipramine: Randomized double-blind study with 135 outpatients

AU: Vorbach-EU; Hubner-WD; Arnoldt-KH

AD: Psychiatrische Klinik im Elisabethenstift, Darmstadt, Germany.

SO: J-Geriatr-Psychiatry-Neurol. 1994 Oct; 7 Suppl 1: S19-23

Description

135 patients, aged 18-75 years, 71 males and 64 females, were given indistinguishable tablets of either hypericum extract LI 160 0.9 mg (standardized hypericin content) x 3 or Imipramine 25 mg x 3 for six weeks in a randomized double-

Table 2 Studies comparing the antidepressant and anxiolytic effect of hypericum to synthetic antidepressants

Authors year	No	substance / Type of study	dose	Hamilton start	end	Other start	end	Resp rate	Stat sign	Side eff	weeks	drop outs	Inclusion criteria
Harrer 1993	44	Jarsin 300	0.9 mg x 3	20.5	12.2	26	16	61%	No	25%	4	17%	ICD 10 F32.1
	42	Maprotilin	25 mg x3	21.5	10.5	25	DS 14	67%	sign	35%		21%	
Bergmann 1993	32	Esbericum	0.25mg x3	15.82	6.34	31.4	24.2	84%	No	24%	6	7%	ICD 10 F32.0, F32.1 F33.0, F33.1
	28	Amitryptilin RCT	10mg x3	15.26	6.65	28.2	DS 24.1	74%	sign	58%		7%	
Vorbach 1993	67	Jarsin 300	0.9 mg x3	20.2	8.8	1.3	3.1	82%	No	12%	6	1.5%	DSM III R, 296.2 296.3, 300.4 309.0
	68	Imipramin	25 mg x3	19.4	10.7	1.2	CGI 2.7	62%	sign	16%		6%	
same	26	same as above	same as above	25	9	-		-	p< 0.05	-	6	-	HAMD >21
	25			24	14								
Werth, 1989	15	Psychotonin	0.37mg c3	24.5	5.0	1.5	2.8	73%	No	7%	3.5	0%	Before and after leg amputation
	15	Imipramin	50 mg x3	26.7	4.7	1.8	CGI 2.5	60%	sign	20%		6.7%	
Kniebel, 1988	65	Sedariston	0.1mg x2*	23.7	5.9	45	16	88%	p< 0.0001	10%	6	1.5%	ICD 09 309.0, 309.1 300.5, 300.4
	65	Amitryptilin	25 mg x3	24.3	7.9	45	DS 22	80%		50%		1.5%	
Warnecke 1986	40	Hyperforat	0.2 mg x3	3.6	2.0	2.8	0.79	77.5%	not made	no serious	12	0%	"climacteric depressions"
	20	Diazepam	2 mg x3	3.8 SDS	2.6	3.0 HAMA	1.9	50.0%				0%	
Panijel, 1985	50	Sedariston	0.1-0.2mg x2*	44.0	11.5	75.5	39.5	78%***	p< 0.0007	4%	2	0%	moderate anxiety syndrome
	50	Diazepam	2-4mg x2	40.0 B-L	22.5	75.5 STAI	53.5	54%***		14%		0%	
Stegr, 1985	93 total	Sedariston	0.1mg x2*	1.0	1.9	25	7	70%	p< 0.0021	no detail	6	0%	light to moderate depressions
		Desipramin	100 mg/day**	1.0 CGI	0.8	27	DS 19	30%				0%	

DS = Depression Scale according to von Zerssen, self-rating, CGI = Clinical Global Impression score, HS = von Zerssen Health Complaint survey

BEB = Symtom complaint inventory, STAI = State Trait Anxiety Inventory, B-L = Beschwerden Liste (Complaint Inventory) according to von Zerssen, SDS =Self Rating Depression Scale , * + 50 mg Valeria, ** First week 150 mg daily, *** Response rate measured by STAI, blind trial.

Inclusion criteria were typical depression according to DSM-III R with a single episode (296.2) or recurrent episodes (296.3), neurotic depression (300.4) and adjustment disorder with depressed mood (309.0).

Exclusion criteria were severe depression requiring inpatient treatment, schizophrenia or marked agitation requiring additional medication; a known history of attempted suicide or acute suicidal state, chronic alcohol and drug dependency and acute confusional state. Use of drugs with cerebral effects, especially psychotropic drugs, was not permitted. In addition, the patients must not have been taking MAO-inhibitors within the previous 2 weeks or drugs for research purposes within the previous 3 months.

There was a washout phase of at least 2 weeks before the start of the study. All non-psychotropic drugs were permitted and recorded on specific data sheets.

The patients had a thorough medical checkup with neurological status and routine Lab-parameters at the start and end of the study.

They were questioned specifically about possible side effects.

Target parameters were the Hamilton Depression Scale (HAMD), the von Zerssen Depression Self-rating Scale (D-S) and the Clinical Global Impressions (CGI).

Compliance was monitored by counting the tablets remaining at every visit. The classification of patients into different diagnostic groups is shown in Table 3.

Results

HAMD score

The mean HAMD fell from 20.2 to 8.8 in the hypericum group and from 19.4 to 10.7 in the Imipramine group.

The reduction of HAMD score was significant with p< 0.001 in both groups. There were no statistically significant differences between the groups.

Figure 1 shows the HAMD-score at entry and after 2, 4 and 6 weeks.

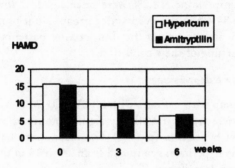

D-S score

The mean D-S score fell from 39.6 to 27. 2 on hypericum and from 39.0 to 29.2 on Imipramine.

CGI score

The CGI score for therapeutic effect rose from 1.3 to 3.1 in the hypericum group and from 1.2 to 2.7 in the Imipramine group.

· The CGI score for change in status was slightly more positive in the hypericum group than in the Imipramine group (see Figure 5); 41% were greatly improved, 35% much improved, 12% slightly better and 12% experienced no change. None of the hypericum patients experienced worsening of their condition. The comparative results for Imipramine were 34% greatly improved, 27% much improved, 17% slightly better, 17% unchanged, 3% somewhat worse and 2% much worse.

The CGI score on change of illness severity also showed a trend towards better results with hypericum. 81.8% were classified as having improved on hypericum while 62.5% had improved on Imipramine. 18.2% were unchanged or the same compared to 34.4% in the Imipramine group. None of the hypericum patients and two of the Imipramine patients experienced worsening of their condition.

Effect on severe depressions

In the subgroup with patients with a HAMD> 21 (severe depressions) there was a statistically significant trend towards superiority of hypericum (p<0.05) The mean score fell from 25 to 9 in the hypericum group and from 24 to 14 in the Imipramine group (see Figure 2).

ADRs

Adverse drug effects (ADRs) occurred in 8 patients on hypericum (11.9%). The most frequent symptoms were dry mouth (4 cases) and dizziness (2 cases). 11 patients mentioned ADRs on Imipramine. The most frequent were dry

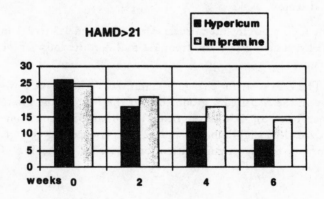

mouth (9 cases), dizziness and anxiety (3 each) and constipation (2 cases). 10 of 11 symptoms were said to be mild with hypericum and 15 were classified as mild, 4 as moderate and 3 as severe on Imipamine (see Table 4).

There were no changes in laboratory parameters or clinical status.

The researchers' comments

The clinical efficacy of Imipramine has been demonstrated in more than 1000 therapeutic studies.

The normal dose of Imipramine for outpatients is 50-150 mg/day. This study used a dose of 75 mg because

1. It is generally agreed upon that 50 mg is a sufficient dose for outpatient treatment, especially with older subjects, who often require lower doses because of slower elimination.

2. With a higher dose there would be a risk that it would be obvious which patients were receiving which drug because of the typical side-effects on Imipramine. This would interfere with the double-blind structure.

This study did show Imipramine to have similar effects and side-effects as in previous studies.

Hypericum was clearly superior to Imipramine in terms of patient tolerance and fewer side effects.

The dose of hypericum was high in this study (2.7 mg hypericin daily). The authors conclude that more studies are needed to determine the dose-response effect with hypericum in order to find the optimum dose of treatment for different conditions.

The finding of superior effect on severe depressions with treatment of hypericum needs to be complemented with more studies on severe depressions and also with comparative studies using higher doses of Imipramine. The Drug Monitoring study by Woelk et al. on 3,250 patients did not show better effect on severe depressions, but that study had a very high proportion of women. In the criteria-based review by Ernst this study scored highest in terms of quality (74 points out of 110).

Study 2

Treatment of mild to moderate depressions: A comparison between *Hypericum perforatum* and Amitryptiline

AU: Bergmann-R, Nuessner-J, Demling-J

SO: Neurologie/Psychiatrie 7, 235-240, vol 4 April 1993

Description

80 patients were treated in a randomized double-blind study for 6 weeks with Esbericum capsules containing 0.25 mg hypericin x 3 or Amitryptilin 10 mg x 3 (a synthetic antidepressant).

- Entrance criteria were mild and moderate depressive syndromes (ICD-10 F32.0 + F32.1) and recurrent depressive episodes of mild to moderate severity (ICD-10 F33.0 + F33.1).

- The patients were also questioned about daily sleep length and dream content.

- Side effect were asked for and recorded.

Results

HAMD

- The mean HAMD fell from 15.82 to 6.34 in the hypericum group and from 15.26 to 6.86 in the

Amitryptiline group.

● The mean HAMD was improved by 60% in the treatment group and 56% in the control group.

● The difference was not statistically significant.

Bf-S

● The mean Bf-s was reduced from 31.45 to 24.22 in the hypericum group and from 28.21 to 24.13 in the control group.

● The difference was not statistically significant.

Dreams and sleep

● Daily sleep amount increased in the hypericum group from 5.60 hours to 6.58 hours and in the Amitryptiline group from 5.51 to 6.73 hours.

● There were no differences observed in quality or quantity of dreams reported between the two groups.

● The amount of anxiety-colored dreams diminished in both groups significantly.

Side effects

● 58% of the patients in the Amitryptiline group complained about tiredness (16 remarks), dry mouth (13 remarks), pressure in the stomach (10 remarks) and a few others about gastrointestinal and respiratory complaints.

● 24% complained about pressure in the stomach, gastric pains and tiredness in the hypericum group.

Dropouts

● 2 persons discontinued the medication in the hypericum group because of gastrointestinal complaints. One of them was given an Amitryptiline preparation after dropping out, which also gave the same problems.

● 2 persons discontinued the study in the Amitryptiline group, reasons were GI symptoms, tiredness and hypomania.

Researchers' comments

The authors noted that placebo-treatment has been found less effective in severe depressions than in mild to moderate depressions.

They suspected that the gastrointestinal complaints in the hypericum group might be more because of the depression than because of side effects from hypericum.

Study 3

Effectiveness and tolerance of hypericum extract LI 160 compared to Maprotiline: A multicenter double-blind study

Au:Harrer-G, Huebner-D, Podzuweit-H

So: J Geriatr Psychiatry Neurol 1994: 7(suppl 1): S24-28

Description

● 102 patients, aged 24-65 years, 29 males and 73 females, were given indistinguishable tablets of either hypericum extract LI 160 0.9 mg (standardized hypericin content) x 3 or Maprotiline 25 mg x 3 for 4 weeks in a randomized double-blind trial.

● Inclusion criteria were depression according to ICD-10 (F32.1) with a single moderately severe depressive episode for at least 2 weeks. The sum of the HAMD with 17 items had to be at least 16.

Results

HAMD score

● The mean HAMD fell from 20.5 to 12.2 in the hypericum group and from 21.5 to 10.5 in the Maprotiline group.

● There were no statistically significant differences between the groups.

● There was a slight difference in favor of Maprotiline after two weeks of treatment (39% decrease compared to 29% with hypericum) treatment, indicating faster effect. The difference diminished after 6 weeks and was no longer significant.

● 61% of the patients fulfilled the response criteria (50% HAMD reduction or HAMD<10) on hypericum and 67% on Maprotiline.

D-S score

● The mean D-S score fell from 26 to 16 on hypericum and from 25 to 14 on Maprotiline.

CGI score

● The CGI score for change in status and severity of illness showed a tendency towards better recovery in the hypericum group. Results are summarized figure 3.

Figure 3 CGI-score change in status

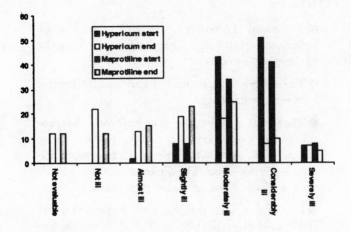

ADRs

Adverse drug effects (ADRs) occurred in 13 patients on hypericum (25%) and on 18 patients on Maprotiline (35%) (see Table 6).

There were no changes in laboratory parameters or clinical status, except for a slight rise in serum creatinine in one patient on Maprotiline (1.1 to 1.8 mg/dl).

Researchers' comments

This study agrees with previous studies comparing Maprotiline, known for its fast effect, and hypericum, known for its benign side-effect profile.

Study 4

Depressive moods

Au: Steger-W

So: Z. Allg. Med. 1985: vol61 pp 914-918

Description

● 93 patients were given either a mixture of valerian and hypericum (Sedariston) or the synthetic antidepressant Desipramine over 6 weeks.

● As measured by the CGI scale, the hypericum group was far superior to the Desipramine group after both 1, 3 and 6 weeks (see Figure11). The hypericum group increased its value from 1.0 to 1.9, while the Desipramine group lowered its value from 1.0 to 0.8.

● 70% of the patients in the trial group had a good or very good benefit-risk response while only 30% of the control group had a good response. The difference was highly statistically significant ($p < 0.0004$) (see figure 4).

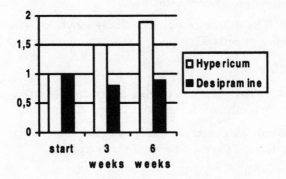

D-S self-report scale on depression

The hypericum group lowered its value from 18 to 4, and the control group from 18 to 9. The difference was statistically significant (p=0.0239) (see Figure 5).

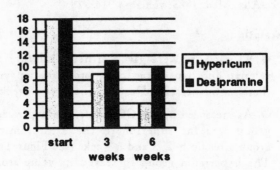

Physical complaint inventory (B-L according to von Zerssen)

● The hypericum group fell from a mean value of 25 at the beginning to 7 at the end.

● The Desipramine group fell from 27 at the beginning to 19 at the end.

● The difference was statistically significant at a value of p=0.0021.

Side effects

● A few patients experienced tiredness, vertigo, tachycardia and dry mouth.

● All side effects were mild and there were no significant differences between the two groups.

● The compliance was good and there where no dropouts because of ADRs.

Researchers' comments

The authors conclude that the combination of hypericum and Valeria is both more effective, better tolerated and has a faster effect than Desipramine.

Our comments

This study is interesting because it is the only one where a herbal combination (hypericum and valeria) has clearly bypassed a conventional antidepressant in terms of efficacy. The superior results of the herbal group over the control group in terms of scales using physical complaints (CGI, Bf-B) versus scales just measuring the psychic parameters (D-S) imply a much more benign side-effect profile as part of the reason for the superiority of the herbal remedy over the synthetic in this study.

The hypericum dose was very low compared to other studies (daily dose 0.20 mg hypericin, in other studies 0.75-2.7 mg daily).

In this study the combination herbal therapy also had a faster effect than the synthetic antidepressant. Most other studies have shown opposite tendencies (with a slower effect of hypericum). This might indicate a potentiating effect of hypericum and valerian. More studies are needed to investigate this, i.e., randomized controlled trials between valerian and hypericum and a combination of both.

The side effects were not well described in this study.

Studies Comparing Hypericum with Placebos

Summary

● There are at least 16 randomized, double-blind studies comparing the antidepressant effect of hypericum extracts to Placebos. There is also one comparing with placebo light therapy.

These studies are summarized in table 3,

● In thirteen of the studies there was a statistically significant difference in efficacy similar to the difference shown between effects of synthetic antidepressants compared to placebos.

● Two of these studies were judged as of low quality (collecting only 25 points out of 110) in terms of reliability concerning methods, patient material and statistical analysis in the systematic, criteria-based review by Ernst. The third one is from a thesis, not yet published in a medical magazine. The study by Osterheider managed to accomplish 0% treatment responses in both placebo and treatment group, a very unusual result. According to informal sources one reason for this very unusual result might have been that a person unknown to the patients did the ratings of depressive symptoms etc., and not their normal doctor. This was not popular among the patients and might have influenced the response rate. In the study by König there were extremely many side-effects, 26% on placebo! There were also many treatment dropouts (25%)

● In no one of the studies here has been any significant difference in terms of ADRs between hypericum and placebo. In a summary of 15 of these studies performed on 1008 patients there was no difference concerning amount of side-effects (4.1% on hypericum and 4.8% on placebo), and actually less treatment dropouts because of side effects among patients treated with hypericum (0.4% versus 1.6%). One can therefore say that hypericum seems to have no significant side effects at all, except for allergic reactions.

● Hypericum has also been proven effective in the treatment of secondary symptoms of depression like headache, sweating, heart palpitations, anxiety and insomnia. There are also promising results in treatment of anxiety syndrome.

Table 3 Summary of studies on Hypericum Vs Placebo

Authors year	No	substance	dose	Hamilton start end		Other start end		Resp rate	Stat sign	Side eff.	weeks	drop outs	Inclusion criteria
Witte 1995	48 49	Psychotonin Placebo	0.5 mg x2	24.6 23	7.9 12	25 21 DS	8 12	79 % 56%	p< 0.02	0 0	6	21% total	ICD10 F32.1
Ditzler 1994	30 30	Nerapas* Placebo	0.24mg3*	15.3 18.4 DS	7.3 12.0	55.7 56.8 DSI	38.4 3.9	67% 33%	p< 0.01	No diff	8	3% 0%	DSM-III-R, major depression,
Sommer 1993	42 47	Jarsin 300 Placebo	0.9 mg x 3	15.8 15.8	7.2 11.3	-		67% 28%	p< 0.01	No diff	4	4% 14%	ICD 09 300.4 309.0
Hübner 1993	20 19	Jarsin 300 Placebo	0.9 mg x 3	12.5 12.4	5 11	15.8 16.7 HS	6.8 16.9	70% 47%	p< 0.05	No diff	4	-	ICD 09 300.4 309.0
König 1993	55 57	extr. Z 90017 Placebo	0.5-1 mgx2	34.7 34.3 B-S	20.8 21.1	64.1 64.7 DSI	48.2 50.6	53% 53%	no diff	22% 28%	6	24% 26%	Psychoaff. disorders with depressed mood
Hänsgen 1993	33 34	Jarsin 300 Placebo	0.9 mg x 3	21.8 20.4	6 14	131 127 BEB	77 104	81% 26%	p< 0.001	6% 3%	6	3% 12%	DSM III R major depression
Lehrl 1993	25 25	Jarsin Placebo	0.37mg x 3	23.7 21.6	17.4 16.8	39.7 41.2 KAI	34.5 37.7	42% 25%	no diff		4	? ?	ICD 09 300.4 309.0
Schmidt 1993	32 33	Jarsin 300 Placebo	0.9 mg x 3	? ?	? ?	No cognitive problems		67% 27%	p< 0.01	7% 10%	6	0%	ICD 09 300,4 309,0
Martinez 1993	10 10	Jarsin 300 + light therapy	300 Lux 3000 Lux	20.6 21.9	8.2 6.1	-		-	No sign	0% 0%	4	0%	DSM III R SAD
Quandt, 1993	88	Psychotonin Placebo	0.37mg x3	17.8 17.3	9.8 16.6	-		71% 7.7%	p< 0.001	0% 0%	4	?	ICD 09 300.4
Osterheider 1992	22 2	Psychotonin Placebo	0.25mg x 3	? ?	? ?	? ?	? ?	0% 0%	No diff	?	8	?	Unspecified Depression

Study	n	Medication	Dose				D-S	%	p	%	n	%	ICD
Reh, 1992	25	Neuroplant	0,5 mg x 2	19	8	30	9 22	80%	p< 0,02	0%	8	0%	ICD 09 300.4 309.0 311.0
	25	Placebo		20	14	32	D-S	44%		0%		0%	
Harrer 1991	58	Psychotonin	0,37 mg x 3	21,6	8,9	11,9	4,5	75%	p< 0,001	2%	6	6,4%	ICD 9 304.4 309.9
	58	Placebo		20,9	16,1	12,1 HAMA	8,2	25%		0%		1,8%	
Halama 1991	25	Jarsin	0,37 mg	18,0	10,0	30,0	12,5	50%	p< 0,005	4 %	4	0%	ICD 09 300.4 309.0
	25	Placebo		17,5	18,0	30,0 B-L	29,5	0%		0%		0%	
Schmidt 1989	16	Psychotonin	0,37 mg x3	29,2	9,7	64,2	51,9	62,%	p< 0,01	0%	4	0%	ICD 09 290.2 296.1 298.0 300.0 300.4
	12	Placebo		29,5	19,5	60,3 STAI	53,1	33,%		0%		0%	
Schlich 1987	22	Psychotonin	0,25 mg x3	22,9	16,4	60,9	19,7	68%	p< 0,05	0%	4	6% total	Unspecified depression
	24	Placebo		24,0	29,6	61,6	55,3	10%		0%		0%	
Hoffman 1979	30	Hyperforat	0,3mg x 3			1,76 own	0,68	61%	not made	0%	6	0%	mild to moderate depression
	30	Placebo				1,83 scale	1,54	16%		0%		0%	

D-S = Depression Scale according to von Zerssen, self-rating, CGI = Clinical Global Impression score, HS = von Zerssen Health Complaint survey, BEB = Symtom complaint inventory, STAI = State Trait Anxiety Inventory, B-L = Beschwerden Liste (Complaint Inventory) according to von Zerssen, HAMA = Hamilton Anxiety scale, DSI = Depression Status Inventory * combination medication with Hypericum, Valeria, Passifiorae, Coridalis cavae and Eschscholixiae californiae

Study 5

Multicenter double-blind study examining the antidepressant effectiveness of the hypericum extract LI 160

Au: Hänsgen-K-D, Vesper-J and Ploch-M

SO: J Geriatr Psychiatry Neurol 1994; (supl1) PP 15-18

Introduction

Previous placebo-controlled, double-blind trials of extract LI 160 have had a duration of 4 weeks, in keeping with the drug trial guidelines for antidepressants. In this study, the trial drug was given for 6 weeks. To enable this, the so-called observation group design was chosen, in which the patients in the placebo group are given the trial medication for the last 2 weeks of the study.

Description

72 patients, aged 18-70 years, with major depression according to DSM-III-R from a total of 11 neurology and psychiatry practices or general practices were given Jarsin 300 (0.9 mg total hypericin) or a placebo for 6 weeks. In weeks 5 and 6, patients in both groups took the trial medication.

Further inclusion criteria were a total score on the Hamilton Depression Scale (HAMD) of 16 or more and a duration of their depressive episode from 2 weeks to a maximum of 6 months.

Patient compliance was evaluated by counting the tablets returned at each follow-up point. Study participants were informed that all patients would receive the trial medication for at least 2 weeks during the course of the study.

Results

● The original placebo group improved in weeks 5 and 6 while on the trial medication, while the treatment group also continued to improve over the same period.

The Hamilton responder rate (reduction of more than 50% in the baseline values, or final scores of less than 10) in week 4 was 81% in the treatment group and 26% in the placebo group.

HAMD score

● Figure 6 shows that the mean fell in the treatment group from a baseline value of 21.8 points to 9.3 points (within the normal range) after 4 weeks, with a further reduction to 6.3 points in weeks 5 and 6, while the placebo group failed to reach normal values. There is a statistically significant difference in this parameter after 2 and 4 weeks (treatment vs placebo, both p <.001).

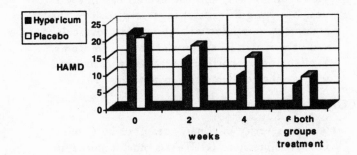

● Subsequent treatment in the placebo group (weeks 5 and 6) also led to a reduction in symptoms, similar to the scaled changes seen in the treatment group in weeks 1 and 2 .

Depression scale (D-S)

● After 4 weeks of treatment with hypericum, normal values were achieved (mean and standard deviation). There were significant differences between groups in weeks 2 and 4 (both p< .001). Subsequent treatment of the placebo group with hypericum (weeks 5 and 6 led to reduction in symptoms, at least as great as those in the treatment group (weeks 1 and 2) when related to the scaled values.

BEB

● The level of symptoms according to the BEB fell in the treatment group from 131 to 89 in week 4 and to 77 in week 6, while in the placebo group it fell from 127 to 104 in week 4 and then, on the trial medication, to 85 points. The groups are different at the 1% level at weeks 2 and 4.

● Figure 7 shows the symptom profile obtained using the BEB in the treatment and placebo groups in week 4, and the overall baseline values. More significant changes are seen in the treatment group for well-being, cardiovascular symptoms, and anxiety/phobia symptoms. Well-being is particularly closely associated with a relief of depressive symptoms.

CGI

● The severity of illness measured by Clinical Global Impressions (CGI) was much reduced after 4 weeks of treatment with the trial drug, with further improvement in the last 2 weeks.

● With the placebo, the severity diminished much less in the first 4 weeks. After that, however, taking the trial medication during the last two weeks

Figure 7

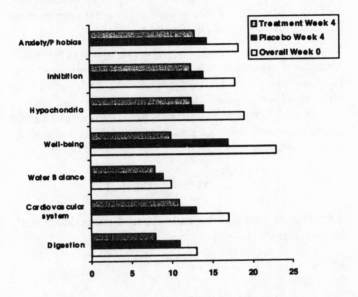

was associated with a noticeable improvement in the placebo group.

Side effects

● One patient in the treatment group complained about sleep disturbance and two in the placebo group complained about gastrointestinal symptoms.

Researchers' comments

In interpreting the results, it must be borne in mind that the participants in the trial knew that they would receive the trial medication for at least 2 weeks. Most of the patients treated with the trial drug benefited from taking hypericum extract, as is shown by the continuous fall in depressive symptoms from the start of the study to the end of week 6 of treatment. Participants in the placebo group had no real improvement in symptoms up to the end of week 4.

Since the influence of certain doctors or practices are eliminated from the overall results because of the large number of practices supplying subjects, the results of a study such as this are particularly powerful. Because of its potent and specific efficacy with few or no side effects, hypericum extract LI 160 can be recommended as an antidepressant for treatment of depressed outpatients.

Study 6

Treatment of mild to moderate depressions with hypericum

AU: Sommer-H; Harrer-G

AD: Psychiatrische Fachpraxis, Universitat Salzburg, Austria.

SO: Phytomedicine Vol. 1/1994, pp 3-8

Description

- In a multicenter randomized double-blind trial, 105 patients aged 20-65 years were given either Jarsin 300 containing 0.9 mg hypericin x 3 or a placebo for four weeks.

- Entrance criteria were neurotic depression (ICD 09 300.4), and brief depressive reaction (ICD 09 309.0).

- All other medical treatments were recorded in order to investigate possible interactions.

Results

● Of the 105 patients included in the study, 9 stopped treatment. Four of them (2 from the trial group and 2 from the placebo group) did not give any reason; 4 from the placebo group stopped because of inefficacy, and one patient in the placebo group stopped because of "undesired side-effects"! Seven patients were excluded before the study started because they no longer fulfilled the inclusion criteria. At the end there were 42 patients in the treatment group and 47 in the placebo group.

● The mean HAMD fell from 15.8 at the beginning to 7.2 at the end in the hypericum group and from 15.8 to 11.3 in the placebo group. The difference was statistically significant with a $p < 0.01$.

● 67% of the patients in the hypericum group were classified as responders, compared to 28% in the placebo group.

● There were impressive improvements concerning depressive mood, difficulty in falling asleep, emotional fear, and psychosomatic symptoms (disturbed sleep, headache, cardiac troubles, exhaustion), but not for feelings of guilt, difficulty in sleeping through and somatic fear in the hypericum group.

● 2 patients in the hypericum group (skin reddening, tiredness) and 3 patients in the placebo group (increased sleep requirement, mild abdominal pains, edema, psychological vulnerability, increase in weight and indecisiveness) experienced adverse drug effects.

● Compliance was good, except for one patient.

● There were no signs of interactions with other pharmaceutical agents.

Researchers' comments

● Dr. Sommer and Harrer emphasize the good compliance with hypericum compared to synthetic antidepressants, which makes it "the remedy of choice" for the treatment of mild to moderate depressions.

● They *do not* recommend hypericum for the treatment of severe depressions, i.e., depressions with suicide risk, psychotic symptoms (delusions, hallucinations) or when the depression seriously disturbs normal work and family life. They unfortunately do not elaborate.

Our comments

● One of many similar studies of the same kind, with very typical results.

● It is interesting to note that ADRs were more common in the placebo group than in the hypericum group. One reason for this could be more somatoform depressive symptoms because of less antidepressant effect.

Study 7

Hypericum in the treatment of seasonal affective disorders

Martinez, S. Kasper, S. Ruhrmann, and H.4. Möller

SO: J Geriatr Psychiatry Neurol 1994; (supl1) PP 29-33

Definitions

Seasonal affective disorder

Seasonal affective disorder (SAD) represents a subgroup of major depression with a regular occurrence of symptoms in autumn/winter and full remission in spring/summer.

A. There is a regular, time-related connection between the onset of an episode of bipolar disturbance (including nonspecified bipolar disturbances) or a major depression (including nonspecified bipolar disturbances) during a certain 60-day period during 1 year (e.g., regular onset of depression between the beginning of October and the end of November).

B. Complete remission (or a change from depression to mania or hypomania) also occurs during a 60-day period in 1 year (e.g., between mid-February and mid-April).

C. At least three episodes of affective disorder have occurred within the last 3 years that exhibit a seasonally dependent relationship as in (A) and (8); in at least 2 successive years.

D. Seasonally dependent episodes of an affective disorder as described above were more frequent than nonseasonal affective disorders (ratio at least 3 to 1).

Light therapy

Light therapy (LT) has become the standard treatment of this type of depression. Light therapy is generally practiced as follows: the light intensity is measured in lux. A standard intensity of 2500 to 3000 lux has proven valuable. This corresponds approximately to the amount of light registered when looking out of a window on a spring day, and is about five times brighter than normal room lighting. The ultraviolet and infrared rays of the very bright, white light emitted are filtered to protect the patient's eyes. The flicker frequency of the lamps is raised electronically to ensure as few adverse effects as possible. This type of phototherapy is applied for 2 hours. The patient is instructed to maintain a distance of around 90 cm from the light, mounted at eye level, and to look into the lamps once a minute. During the treatment session, the patient can perform any sitting tasks, such as paperwork. The time of day at which light is applied does not appear to be essential, although there are indications that the morning is more beneficial. As a rule, phototherapy must he applied without interruption during the critical season, because premature discontinuation results in remanifestation of symptoms. Apart from this, pharmacotherapy with antidepressants also seems to provide an improvement of SAD symptoms. The aim of this study was to check whether hypericum has any effect on SAD.

Description

Twenty SAD patients (13 women and 7 men) who fulfilled DSM-III-R criteria for major depression with seasonal pattern were randomized in a 4-week treatment study and were given 900 mg of Jarsin 300 (2.7 mg hypericin) per day combined with either bright (3000 lux, n 10) or dim (<300 lux, n 10) light. Light therapy was applied for 2 hours daily. The length of the study was 4 weeks.

The clinical efficacy was evaluated on the basis of the following parameters: Hamilton Depression Scale, 21-item version (HAMD), Supplementary HAMD scale, Hypomania scale (HY), Expectation Scale (ES), Profile of Mood States (POMS), the von Zerssen Self-Rating Scale (Bf-S), von Zerssen's Depression Scale (D-S), and Visual Analog scales.

Results

● At the onset of treatment, all patients reported that they were extremely tired, and 92% had depressive moods. Anxiety occurred in 81% of the patients, 55% had noticed that they were less active, and 46% had an increased appetite. Similarly, libido was weaker in 46%, and 71% stated that they slept longer.

● The seasonal fluctuations in mood were recorded quantitatively using the Seasonal Pattern Assessment Questionnaire. The 20 patients in our trial felt they were worse in November, December, and January (90% to 95%) and at their best during the months of May, June, July, and August (70% to 100%).

● The sum score of the Hamilton Depression Scale (HAMD) was comparable for both groups (hypericum + bright light and hypericum + dim light) before treatment (Figure 16). During the 4-week treatment period, the group with hypericum + bright light showed a drop in the HAMD sum score of 72% (21.9 to 6.1), and the group with hypericum + dim light a drop in score of 60% (20.6 to 8.2).

● There was a statistically significant effect of treatment in both groups (p = 0.001)

● There was no significant difference in treatment effect between the two groups.

● Analysis of the self-rating scales (POMS; Bf-S; D-S) showed no significant difference between the two groups.

● A significant decrease in symptomatology was recorded for the whole group during the 4 weeks of treatment for all the POMS factors: despondency (p = .0001); fatigue (p = .0001); desire for action (p =.0001); and bad temper (p = .0001).

● None of the patients in either treatment group reported any adverse drug reactions.

Researchers' comments

These results, which were gained from a relatively small sample, show that hypericum also has antidepressive actions in SAD patients. This is important insofar as this was the first trial ever to investigate the effectiveness of hypericum in SAD patients.

Nevertheless, the results support the assumption that the antidepressant effect of hypericum might be increased by the additional application of phototherapy. Equally, there were no indications that combined therapy takes effect more quickly. However, since a smaller number of patients were enrolled in this trial, it is conceivable that the absence of a difference is attributable to the small sample size. Thus, in order to provide conclusive answers to this question as well as the question of efficacy, trials on larger subject groups, including a placebo group, are necessary. Still, if these preliminary results are confirmed, namely that hypericum also has antidepressive effects in SAD patients, this would represent an alternative form of treatment to phototherapy, regarded by some patients as too time consuming.

Our comments

● This study seems to confirm the possibility that hypericum has a light sensitizing mechanism, as referred to in the study, "Nocturnal Melatonin and Cortisol Secretions Before and After Subchronic Administration of Hyperforat."

Study 8

Antidepressant treatment with hypericin

Au: Hoffman-J, Kuehl-E-D

So: Z allg. Med. 55, 776-782(1979)

Introduction

The authors report that hypericin, in addition to its antidepressive properties, also has a good effect on the circulatory system because of an increase of capillary circulation.

Asselhuber et al. have a found a good effect on Enuresis nocturna (bed-wetting).

There are also clinical reports of good effect on psychosomatic symptoms in children and migraine.

Description

60 patients aged 19-73 years (31 men, 29 women) were given 25-30 Hyperforat drops (containing approximately 3 mg hypericin) or a placebo three times a day before meals in a randomized, double-blind study for six weeks.

The trial group had 5 mild, 23 moderate and 4 severe depressions,

The control group 4 mild, 22 moderate and 4 severe depressions.

The symptoms were measured with a scale containing 52 symptoms graded from 0 = no complaints to 3 = serious complaints. The measurements were made in the beginning, after three weeks and after six weeks.

Results

⬤ The mean value of symptoms fell from 1.76 at the start to 1.16 after three weeks and 0.68 after six weeks in the hypericum group.

⬤ The scores in the placebo group were 1.83 at the beginning, 1.63 after three weeks and 1.54 after six weeks.

⬤ The response rate was 34.1% after three weeks and 61.4% after six weeks in the trial group and 10.9% after three weeks and 15.8% after six weeks in the placebo group.

- When measured by 19 of the more "depressive complaints," the response rate was even higher (70%). The response rate was 18.9% in the placebo group with this scale.

- When measured as good/very good response 63% had a good effect in the trial group and 10% on the placebo, while 20% on hypericum and 67% on the placebo were classified as nonresponders.

- There were slightly better results with juvenile and climacteric depressions, than with psychogene, somatogene, and involution depressions.

There were no statistical analyses made.

No side effects reported, either by clinical or laboratory investigations. No drop outs.

Our comments

This study is the oldest we know of and there was no statistical analysis and a scale not widely tested and used in other circumstances. It was also before the age of DSM III and all the modern classifications. We brought it into this summary mostly because it was the first ever performed on hypericum and thus is of historical interest.

Study 9

Hypericum extract in the treatment of depression: An effective alternative

Au: Reh C, Laux P, Schenk N. :

So: Therapiewoche 1992; 42:1576-81

Description

50 patients aged 20-65 years were given either two capsules

of Neuroplant (25 mg total hypericin each) two times a day or a placebo for eight weeks.

Entrance criteria were neurotic depression (ICD 09 300.4), brief depressive reaction (ICD 09 309.0) and other unclassified depressive states (ICD 311.0).

Target parameters were the Hamilton Depression scale (HAMD), the Hamilton Anxiety scale (HAMA), the Clinical Global impression scale (CGI) and the von Zerssen self-rating scale (D-S).

Results

The mean HAMD fell from 19 at the beginning to 8 at the end in the hypericum group and from 20 to 14 in the placebo group. The difference was statistically significant with a p< 0.02.

80% of the patients in the hypericum group were classified as responders according to HAMD, compared to 44% in the placebo group.

The mean D-S fell from 30 at the beginning to 9 at the end in the hypericum group and from 32 to 22 in the placebo group.

- The mean HAMA was lowered by 70% in the hypericum group and 42.1% in the placebo group.

- According to the CGI, 90% of the hypericum group and 55% of the placebo group got better.

- The results after eight weeks were much better than after four weeks.

No side effects were noted in either group.

Our comments

This study lasted eight weeks. More than 50% of the effect came between weeks four and eight. This implies that long-term studies may show hypericum to be even more effective, and that no one has yet seen when the effect of hypericum fades out, as even in this study, the results continued to get better from week 6 to 8.

Drug Monitoring Studies

Summary

Drug monitoring studies are made in order to collect knowledge on licensed drugs on a large scale. Drug monitoring studies usually allow inclusion of a much greater number of patients than controlled clinical studies and are thus primarily of use in establishing side effects, but may also predict efficacy, especially in different age groups or with different severity of illness.

As far as we know, there have been two drug-monitoring studies performed so far: one on 3,250 patients taking the high-dose preparation Jarsin 300 and one on 1,040 patients taking the low-dose preparation Jarsin.

Results are summarized in Table 4.

Table 4. Summary of 2 drug monitoring studies studies on the efficiency and safety of Hypericum in the treatment of depression.

Authors year	No	sub stance	dose	Hamilton start	end	DS - scale start	end	Resp rate	Side eff.	we eks	drop outs	Inclusion criteria
Albrecht 1994	1060	Jarsin	0.37mg x3	18.4	5.4	21.1	7.3	93%	2%	4	5.9%	ICD 10 F32.1
Woelk 1993	3250	Jarsin 300	0.9 mg x3			23.2	11.8	82%	2.4%	4	1.5%	Mild, mode-rate and severe dep.

Study 10

Benefits and risks of the hypericum extract LI 160: Drug-monitoring study with 3,250 patients

AU: Woelk-H; Burkard-G; Grunwald-J

AD: Psychiatrisches Landeskrankenhaus und Akademisches Lehrkrankenhaus, Universitat Giessen, Germany.

SO: J-Geriatr-Psychiatry-Neurol. 1994 Oct; 7 Suppl 1: S34-8

Description

Effectiveness and acceptance of a 4-week treatment with hypericum extract LI 160 Jarsin 300 (=3x 0.9 mg total hypericin) were investigated by 663 private practitioners. The results of the 3,250 patients (76% women and 24% men), were recorded using data sheets. Eight typical symptoms were recorded (see Figures 12 and 13). Severity of depression was measured with von Zerssen's D-S self-rating schedule. The severity and duration of all possible side effects were also recorded. Finally the doctor and patients evaluated the course of treatment together, rating the patient's condition as either worse, unchanged, better, symptom-free (see Figure 10). The different specialties of the physicians involved are summarized in Table 5.

Table 5

Specialty	Number	%
Total	3250	100%
General medicine	2471	76%
General practice	730	23%
Neurologists/psychiatrists	91	14%
Internal medicine	84	13%
Others	72	11%

Results

General improvements

The proportion of improvement in depressive and somatic symptoms was similar to other studies on hypericum. About 80% of the patients felt better and 15% unchanged or worse when asked to make an overall judgment. Figure 9 shows these results.

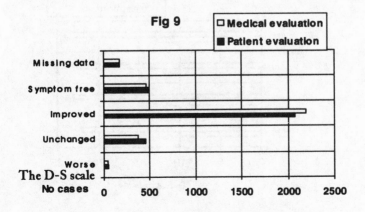

Fig 9
□ Medical evaluation
■ Patient evaluation

The D-S scale

All side effects were mild and there were no significant differences between the two groups. When measured with the D-S scale, the response rate was between 60% and 70%. Figures 10 and 11 show the results on the D-S scale according to severity of symptoms and different age groups.

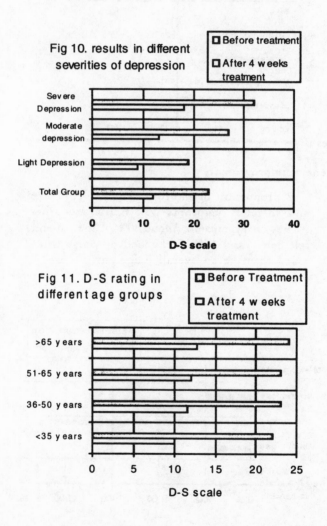

Severity and frequency of symptoms

All side effects were mild and there were no significant differences between the two groups. It was found that the majority of patients got better, but only a small proportion achieved complete freedom from symptoms. Figure 12 shows the frequencies in percent of the symptoms mentioned. Figure 13 shows the corresponding severity of symptoms.

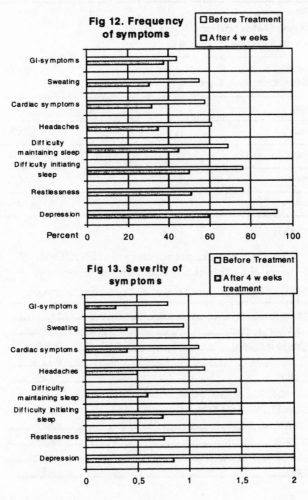

Side effects

Side effects were rare (seen in only 2.4% of the subjects) and mild. Table 6 shows the most common spontaneously mentioned side effects.

Table 6 Spontaneously Mentioned Side effects of Treatment

side-effect	number	percent
GI-symptoms (nausea 6, abdominal pains 5, loss of appetite 3, diarrhea 2, general GI 2)	18	0.55%
Allergic reactions (allergy 6, skin rash 6, pruritus 5)	17	0.52%
Fatigue	13	0.40%
Anxiety	8	0.26%
Dizziness	5	0.15%
Other	18	0.55%
Total	79	2.43%

Dropouts

The dropout frequency was 1.45%. Table 7 shows the reasons for dropouts in this study.

Table 7 Reasons for a Total of 48 Treatment Dropouts

Reason	Number	Percent
Inadequate effect	11	0.34%
Allergic reactions	10	0.30%
GI-symptoms	4	0.12%
Dizziness	4	0.12%
Worsening of concomitant conditions	3	0.09%
Freedom from symptoms	3	0.09%
Anxiety	2	0.06%
Fatigue	2	0.06%
Other reasons	9	0.27%
Total	48	1.45%

Researchers' comments

All side effects were mild and there were no significant differences between the two groups. For evaluation of side effects, it is important to mention that about 50% of the patients already had "gastrointestinal symptoms" before the study. Anxiety, fatigue and dizziness are also frequently associated with depression. It is therefore very hard to scientifically conclude whether these "side effects" were due to depression or were because of the treatment with hypericum.

- From personal contact with one of the researchers we have heard that the "allergic reactions" (0.5%) where pure allergic reactions and did not have any relationship with the photosensitizing effect of hypericum.

- The responder rates in this study are similar to those made on synthetic antidepressants, although a placebo response of 30% can be expected. The results also correspond to the other responder rates in other studies on hypericum.

- Mild and moderate depressions seem to respond equally well in this study.

- The somewhat reduced efficacy in the severe forms contrasts to the findings of Huebner et al. on depressions with HAMD>21. One reason for this discrepancy could be the small number of severe depressions included in this study.

- Efficacy seems not to correlate with age to any greater extent.

The side-effect rate was only 2.4%, compared to 19% in a similar study on Fluoxethine (Prozac).

The dropout rate was about five times lower than in similar studies performed on "the new generation" synthetic anti-depressants.

Our comments

Our clinical experience indicates that side effects on synthetic antidepressants are much more prevalent than on hypericum.

Our experience is that loss of sexual interest, orgasm and impotence problems are far more frequent, but are underreported in many clinical studies for the following reasons:

● Many doctors and patients hesitate to speak about these things and it requires quite a lot of confidence and trust for most patients to be able to open up about these issues.

● Many patients might not have a partner, might have been abusing sex as a way to escape their depression or might have severe guilt feelings about their sexuality and sexual fantasies. For these patients, reduced sexual drive can be a release. They might feel happy to "not be slaves of their hormones." Is lack of sexual desire a side effect or a desired effect in these cases?

Pharmaceutical Studies

Summary

Medical researchers tend to claim that they know more than they actually do. We really do not know how antidepressants work. There are still many black holes in our knowledge and there will certainly be many revisions about how they and hypericum exert their effect. For example, nobody has, as far as we know, yet come up with a good explanation for why it often takes so long for antidepressants to start working.

Hypericum was first thought to be a MAO-inhibitor, but today the most popular hypotheses are that hypericum works through cytokine modulation and serotonin and norepinephrine reuptake inhibition. We are quite sure this is not yet the end of the story. One hypothesis is that hypericum acts on many levels simultaneously, creating an accumulating effect by being both a MAO-inhibitor, serotonin-, norepinephrine-, and dopamine-reuptake inhibitor, a cortisol secretion inhibitor, etc. ("Many small streams create a great river.")

Is it possible that the different types of action harmonize together, to create a maximum amount effect at a certain point, with a minimum of side-effects, just like when the different rays from sunlight converge through a lens to create intense heat at the focus-point?

There are many studies documenting the clinical antidepressant effect of hypericum and it can be concluded that hypericum possesses an antidepressant effect of a magnitude similar to synthetic antidepressants, but with a minimum of side effects.

Hypericin accumulates in brain, stomach and skin tissue, but is more rapidly excreted in other tissues. This might be an explanation to its benign effect-side-effect profile and why its primary sites of action have been in the brain, skin and GI-system. (The most common side-effect complaints have come from these areas.)

● In a recent study Müller et al. have demonstrated a norepinephrine- and serotonin-reuptake-inhibiting effect of hypericum extract. It remains to be established whether this has clinical effect, as the concentrations of the active ingredients of hypericum in the human brain during antidepressive treatment has not been established.

Another hypothesis is that hypericum acts on the CRH, ACTH and cortisol system by inhibiting the cytokine interleukin-6 and other cytokines excreted by cells of the immune-system.

● There are also interesting investigations on hypericum's effect on urinary secretion of catecholamine metabolites, light-induced and nocturnal secretion of melatonin and effects on benzodiazepine receptors.

There are also interesting findings on the dopamine- reuptake inhibiting and prolactin-inhibiting effects of hypericum extract by Winterhoff et al.

● We will also report on the pharmacokinetics and pharmacological properties of hypericum extract in this section.

Study 11

Pharmacokinetics of hypericin and pseudohypericin after oral intake of the *Hypericum perforatum* extract LI 160 in healthy volunteers

AU: Staffeldt-B; Kerb-R; Brockmoller-J; Ploch-M; Roots-I

AD: Institut fur Klinische Pharmakologie, Universitatsklinikum Charite Berlin, Germany.

SO: J-Geriatr-Psychiatry-Neurol. 1994 Oct; 7 Suppl 1: S47-53

Setup

The single- and multiple-dose pharmacokinetics of hypericin and pseudohypericin were studied in 12 healthy malesubjects. After a single oral dose of 300, 900, or 1800 mg of dried hypericum extract (250, 750, or 1500 micrograms hypericin and 526, 1578, or 3156 micrograms pseudohypericin and 900, 2700, and 5400 microg. total hypericin), plasma levels were measured up to 3 days.

Some facts about the flower *Hypericum perforatum* and its content of hypericin

The hypericum extract was taken from the upper parts of *Hypericum perforatum* L just before or during the blossoming. It has been found that the concentrations of hypericin can vary with a factor of 10 between individual plants.

Table 8 gives a summary of the contents and concentration of important substances in a selection of the blooms of 50 hypericum plants.

Table 8

Constituent	Content in %
Hypericine	0.086
Pseudohypericin	0.23
Hyperforin	2.80
Biapigenin	0.26
Rutin	0.28
Hyperoside	0.66
Isoquercitrin	0.31
Quercitrin	0.34

Results

● The median maximal plasma levels were 1.5, 4.1, and 14.2 ng/ml for hypericin and 2.7, 11.7, and 30.6 ng/ml for pseudohypericin, respectively, for the three doses given above (interim evaluation of four volunteers).

● The median elimination half-life times of hypericin were 24.8 to 26.5 hours, and varied for pseudohypericin from 16.3 to 36.0 hours.

● Ranging between 2.0 to 2.6 hours, the median lag-time of absorption was remarkably prolonged for hypericin when compared to pseudohypericin (0.3 to 1.1 hours).

● The areas under the curves (AUC) showed a nonlinear increase with raising dose; this effect was statistically significant for hypericin.

● During long-term dosing (3 x 300 mg/day), a steady-state was reached after 4 days.

● Mean maximal plasma level during the steady-state treatment was 8.5 ng/ml for hypericin and 5.8 ng/ml for pseudohypericin, while mean trough levels were 5.3 ng/ml for hypericin and 3.7 ng/ml for pseudohypericin.

● In spite of their structural similarities, there are substantial pharmacokinetic differences between hypericin and pseudohypericin.

Study 12

Hypericin uptake in rabbits and nude mice transplanted with human squamous cell carcinomas: Study of a new sensitizer for laser phototherapy

AU: Chung-PS; Saxton-RE; Paiva-MB; Rhee-CK; Soudant-J; Mathey-A; Foote-C; Castro-DJ

AD: Department of Otolaryngology-Head and Neck Surgery, Dankook University, College of Medicine,

Cheonan, Korea.

SO: Laryngoscope. 1994 Dec; 104(12): 1471-6

Description

Tissue uptake and biodistribution of hypericin were measured in rabbits and in mice xenografted with P3 human squamous cell carcinoma to assess the value of this dye as an in vivo sensitizer for laser photoactivation of solid tumors. Rabbits were examined after 4 and 24 hours; mice were examined after 2, 4, 6, 8, and 24 hours and after 3 and 7 days for dye uptake in different organ systems.

Results

● The peak concentration of hypericin in the mice's organs was reached at 4 hours with uptake per gram of tissue as follows: lung > spleen > liver > blood > kidney > heart > gut > tumor > stomach > skin > muscle > brain.

● There was approximately 35 times higher uptake of hypericin in lung tissue compared to the brain.

● The elimination of hypericin was rapid in most mouse organs with residual dye under 10% of maximum after 7 days, compared to 25% to 33% retention in brain, skin and stomach, indicating a possibility of accumulation in brain and skin tissue over time (see Figure 14).

Figure 14. Hypericin retention in % of maximum uptake after 7 days in different murine organs.

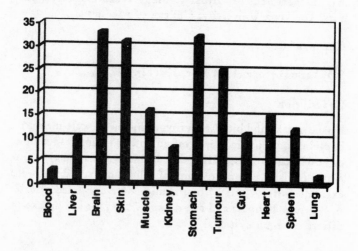

● The authors therefore suggest that hypericin may be a useful photosensitizer for photodynamic therapy of human cancer.

Comments

Does hypericine pass the blood-brain-barrier?

One of the unclear issues has been whether hypericum passes the blood-brain-barrier (BBB).

Thiele et al. have postulated that hypericin does not pass the BBB, and thus must have its primary site of action outside of the CNS. This study clearly contradicts this. It is demonstrated that hypericin passes over to the brain in mice and rabbits, but in very small concentrations. The concentration in brain tissue is only 20 ng/ml four hours after intravenous injection of hypericin in a dose of 1 mg. The blood concentration was at maximum 400 ng/ml.

The concentration in spleen and lungs was 500-700 ng/ml.

Accumulation of hypericin in brain tissue

The really interesting fact is that the elimination of hypericin in brain tissue (and skin and stomach—organs where hypericine is supposed to have good effect)—seems to be extremely slow. The exact half-life of hypericin in brain tissue was not clearly determined, but the diagrams suggest that it might be several weeks! Is this the reason why hypericum has such a slow, steadily increasing effect on depression? It seems likely that the brain concentration of hypericin will continue to rise for a long time until it reaches a steady state. This needs to be further investigated in animal experiments.

Hypericum sales in Germany unknown in America

The authors conclude that hypericin also has an antidepressant effect, but state that it is no longer used as in anti-depressive treatment. At the same time the study was done, hypericum had 30% of the German antidepressant market.

Study 13

Pharmacological profile of hypericum extract: Effect on serotonin uptake by postsynaptic receptors

AU: Perovic-S and Mueller-W-E-G

SO: Arzneimittel-Forschung/Drug Research 45 (II), 11, 1145-1148(1995)

Description

Brains from adult rats were dissected on ice, cortices homogenized and centrifuged in an established way that results in a separation of postsynaptic membranes and an enrichment of postsynaptic receptors. This synaptosomes were then incubated together with hypericum extract LI 160 in different concentrations. Uptake was initiated by an addition of 5 micromol of radioactive serotonin and terminated by dilution on ice buffer and rapid filtration through glass fiber filters. The incubation period was 0-30 minutes. Radioactivity on filters was measured by liquid scintillation spectrometry. To correct for passive transport, the uptake at 0-4 degrees Celsius was measured.

Summary

● It was concluded that hypericum extract LI 160 inhibits serotonin uptake into rat synaptosomes in vitro, thus increasing the concentration of serotonin in the synapse.

● The reuptake inhibition shows an almost linear dose-response curve, with 20% inhibition at a hypericum concentration of 0.3 microg/ml, 50% at 6.2 microg/ml and 90% inhibition at a dose of 20 mikrog/ml.

Comments

The concentration necessary for a 50% inhibition was 6.2 microg/ml .This is equivalent to a concentration of hypericin of 6200 ng/m l (the dose in ngrams) x 0.25 mg (amount of hypericin in 300 mg extract) divided with 300 mg = 5.2 ng. That corresponds roughly to a fourth of the concentration measured in the brain after injection of 1 mg/kg hypericin in mice in the study by Chung et al. The blood level was 400 ng/ml in that same experiment. The mean steady-state concentration in blood for patients treated with 0,9 mg hypericin x 3 daily per os was measured to be 5.3 ng /ml, which is approximately 80 times lower than in the mice described above. This means that the probable level needed to get an immediate 50% reduction of serotonin uptake in the brain would be 80/4= 20 times that used in antidepressant treatment. What might be able to explain the possible effects is the accumulation of hypericin in the brain described in the study by Chung et al. For a final evaluation of Perovic and Mueller's findings, it is necessary to establish the concentration of hypericin in the human brain in patients treated with hypericum extract.

Treatment with high initial doses?

It might be intelligent to change the policy of antidepressive treatment, to start treatment with very high dosages initially in order to reach steady-state concentrations sooner. This could be a subject for future trials.

Accumulation in brain tissue as an explanation of benign side-effect profile?

The accumulation of hypericin in the brain over time might also explain why hypericum has such a benign effect-side-effect profile compared to other antidepressants. The slow accumulation in the brain leaves other areas in the body less exposed to possible effects on the serotonin metabolism in other parts of the body.

Clinical studies on long-term effect are needed

Due to hypericum's slow accumulation in the brain, we recommend studies on the long-term effects of treatment with hypericum.

Study 14

St. John's wort: In-vitro study about hypericum extract, hypericin and kampferol as antidepressants

Au: Müller W.E. and Schäfer C.S

Deutsche Apotheker Zeitung vol 136 Nr 13 1996 page 1015-1022

Description

In this study the reuptake of norepinephrine and serotonin in rat brains is studied. The methods are similar to Study 13 above.

The effect of these substances on the so-called imipramine receptor is also studied.

Results

They found that hypericum extract at a concentration of 15 microg/ml reduced the synaptosomal reuptake of both norepinephrine and serotonin by 50%. This result is not very far from the result in the previously mentioned study (6 microg/ml) that used a slightly different method. As comparison, a concentration 20 microg / ml only led to a MAO-inhibition of 20%.

Pure hypericin and pure Kampferol did not have as much effect as the full hypericum extract. It therefore seems obvious that these substances alone do not explain the effect of hypericum.

Researchers' comments

Because we do not know the therapeutic concentrations in the brain of the leading substances in hypericum extract and which substances make the effect, it is hard to conclude whether or not these results explain how hypericum works. More research is needed.

Our comments

It seems likely that hypericum works on both norepinephrine and serotonin reuptake. The 20% inhibition of MAO on a concentration of 20 microg/ml might not be able to explain hypericum's antidepressant effect by itself, but might contribute to the serotonin and norepinephrine reuptake inhibiting effect. Recent studies have confirmed that a combination of serotonin reuptake inhibitors and MAO-inhibitors can be very powerful, even at low concentrations.

Study 15

Inhibition of MAO and COMT by hypericum extracts and hypericin

AU: Thiede-HM; Walper-A

AD: AnalytiCon Gesellschaft fur Chemische Analytik und Consulting mbH, Berlin, Germany.

SO: J-Geriatr-Psychiatry-Neurol. 1994 Oct; 7 Suppl 1: S54-6

Introduction

Depression is associated with changes in levels of the neurotransmitters serotonin and norepinephrine, which are broken down by the enzymes mono-amino-oxidase (MAO) and catechol-O-methyl-transferase (COMT). It has been demonstrated that an inhibition of these enzymes has an antidepressant effect by lowering the breakdown, thus increasing the concentration of these neurotransmitters in the synapses between the nerve cells.

In 1978 Suzuki et al. demonstrated an irreversible MAO-inhibitory effect of hypericum extract; for a long time this was assumed to be the explanation for the antidepressant action of hypericum.

Later research has not been able to confirm this hypothesis; this study was done in order to further investigate the role of MAO and COMT in the antidepressant action of hypericum extracts.

Description

The influence of hypericin, hypericum total extract, and hypericum fractions on the activity of MAO and COMT, prepared in vitro from pork liver, were investigated in several concentration steps.

Results

An inhibition of MAO could be shown in the following concentrations (extract correlated to a mean molecular value of 500): hypericin to 10(-3) mol/L(= 500 microg/ml = unbelievably high in a human brain), hypericum total extract to 10(-4) mol/L, one extract fraction up to 10(-5). A COMT inhibition could not be shown for hypericin, with hypericum extract to 10(-4) mol/L and with two extract fractions also up to 10(-4) mol/L. The MAO-inhibition fraction contained hypericins as well as flavonols, the COMT-inhibition fraction being mainly flavonols and xanthones.

Conclusion

The concentrations of inhibition, particularly MAO activity, shown might not be sufficient to explain the clinically proven antidepressive effect of hypericum.

Study 16

Modulation of cytokine expression by hypericum extract

AU: Thiele-B; Brink-I; Ploch-M

AD: Medizinische Fakultat (Charite) der Humboldt Universitat zu Berlin, Germany.

SO: J-Geriatr-Psychiatry-Neurol. 1994 Oct; 7 Suppl 1: S60-2

Introduction

Recent research suggests that except for the well known role of neurotransmitters like serotonin and norepinephrine, there might also be other important physiological mechanisms involved in the patophysiology of depression.

One of these is the possible indirect actions via the immune system.

The immune system and the nervous system are the only known biological structures possessing a memory capacity.

How these memory functions actually work is still largely unknown, but we know that there is a lot of interaction between the CNS and the immune system. Part of this is due to production and secretion of certain molecules, including endorphins, ACTH (adreno-cortico-trope hormone), ADH (antidiuretical hormone) and in particular certain cytokines. Cytokines are heavily involved in the communication between cells inside and outside the immune system, especially in the nervous system. Virtually all systematic manifestations of immune system activation are mediated either directly or indirectly by the brain or the endocrine organs. Activation of the immune system is causally associated with extensive changes in neural and/or endocrine functions.

These changes include fever, somnolence, loss of appetite, activation of the hypothalamic-hypophyseal-adrenal axis and suppression of the hypothalamic-hypophyseal-gonadal axis and that of the hypothalamic-hypophyseal-thyroid.

It cannot be ruled out that, in subjects with an appropriate disposition, monocyteinterleukins (monokines) are capable of inducing all the signs of depressive illness. According to this hypothesis, a large variety of white blood mononuclear cells (stimulated by infection, allergy, estrogen) would lead to increased levels of interleukins, resulting in changes in mental state.

The aim of this pilot study was to determine whether hypericum extract LI 160 exerts effects on the immune system in vitro, compatible with the "mediator theory" of its antidepressant effect.

Description

The effect of hypericum extract LI 160 on the stimulated cytokine expression was investigated in vitro in a whole blood culture system on non-immune-stimulated cells and on cells stimulated by phytohemagglutinin (PHA) or lipopolysaccharides (LPS). Blood samples were taken from five healthy volunteers and four depressive patients.

The release of the cytokines interleukin-6 (IL-6), interleukin-1 beta (IL-1 beta) and tumor necrosis factor-alpha (TNF-alpha) was measured quantitatively after an incubation time of 24 hours on microtiter plates.

The hypericin concentration was 2 microl/200 microl = 10 microl/ml = 10mg/ml =120 000 ng/ml hypericin.

Steady state concentration of hypericin during treatment with hypericin was measured to 5 ng/ml by Staffeldt et al.

Results

- IL-6 levels in the stimulated group were significantly and almost completely suppressed by hypericum, both in healthy and depressed subjects.

- IL-1B and TNF-a were less affected.

- There was no effect on nonstimulated cells (i.e., under resting conditions)

- Mononuclear cells showed a different reaction pattern in their cytokine production after stimulation with PHA or LPS when exposed to hypericum extract.

- Two of the four patients with depression and none of the healthy subjects showed suppression of production and release of IL-1B in the presence of hypericin compared to controls.

Researchers' comments

Cytokines affect the nervous system both directly and indirectly.

IL-1 had the following direct effects:

- prolongation of slow-wave sleep, appetite loss

- inhibition of gastric acid and gastric secretion

- a strong analgesic component

- a central inhibition of GRH, TRH, vasopressin and oxytocin.

IL-1B and IL-6 have the following effects:

- induced CRH, ACTH and cortisol production

● CRH in turn stimulates the production of IL-6; thus a vicious circle can be created.

Other facts:

● Patients with depression often have an over-secretion of CRH

● Patients with depression also seem to have a reduced amount of central CRH receptors.

Hypericum appears to reduce the interleukin-6 excretion, which in turn reduces the CRH, ACTH and corticosteroid secretion.

Study 17

Effects of hypericum extract on the expression of serotonin receptors

AU: Mueller-WE; Rossol-R

AD: Institute fur Physiologische Chemie der Johannes-Gutenberg-Universitat, Mainz, Germany.

SO: J-Geriatr-Psychiatry-Neurol. 1994 Oct; 7 Suppl 1: S63-4

Description

The influence of hypericum extract LI 160 on the expression of serotonin receptors was investigated using a neuroblastoma cell line to establish a model for the regulation of neurotransmitters by immunologically active compounds such as cytokines. The cells were incubated with hypericum extract LI 160 in kinetic form for 2, 4, 6, 8, and 10 hours, then washed. The hypericum concentrations were 5 x 0.0001 to 5 x 0.000001 mol/l = 50-0.5 microg/ml extract = 6-600 ng/ml hypericine = within the range for possible hypericum concentrations in the brain during antidepressant treatment. The serotonin receptor expression analysis was compared to that of a placebo control solution.

Results

The neuroblastoma cells showed a clearly reduced expression of the serotonin receptors under treatment with hypericum extract. The first stimulation experiments with interleukin-1 (IL-1) and hypericum extract suggest that a further reduction of the serotonin receptors is possible when IL-1 is added.

Researchers' comments

The reduced serotonin receptor availability might inhibit the reuptake ability of serotonin into the cells.

Unlike classic antidepressants, which bind the neurotransmitter, hypericum might "block" the entry point back into the cells, leading to an increased level of neurotransmitters and by that an antidepressant effect.

The influence of hypericum on IL-1 might also contribute to a stronger serotonin reuptake inhibition.

Study 18

Pharmaceutical quality of hypericum extracts

AU: Wagner-H; Bladt-S

AD: Institute fur Pharmazeutische Biologie der Universitat Munchen, Germany.

SO: J-Geriatr-Psychiatry-Neurol. 1994 Oct; 7 Suppl 1: S65-8

Summary

● Hypericum extracts contain at least ten constituents or groups of components that may contribute to the pharmacological effects. It is not yet possible to correlate the antidepressive mode of action with specific constituents; therefore, the pharmaceutical quality of the extracts was characterized on the basis of typical leading substances and especially the hypericins.

● The red-colored hypericins have been found in very few other plants, while most other ingredients are found in many other plants.

● The hypericins also have a photodynamic effect, and sometimes they do not occur until the crude drug has been processed and exposed to light. The concentration of hypericins (mainly hypericine and pseudohypericin) in buds and flowers can vary between 0.06% and 0.75%. A minimum content of 0.04% total hypericin is required for commercial qualities.

● For the analysis and improvement of the production procedure, the content of hypericin and pseudohypericin was measured experimentally. The drug material was extracted with different solvents and the yield was analyzed for each kind of solvent, its concentration and extraction temperature. Optimal yields were obtained with 80% methanol at temperatures of 80 degrees C.

Table 9 shows the percentages of hypericin and pseudohypericin obtained with different extract solutions.

Solvent	Hypericine %	Pseudo-Hypericine %
Methanol	75%	80%
Ethanol	34%	37%
Acetone	20%	20%
Isopropanol	10%	10%
Water	10-20%	30-40%

Study 19

Nocturnal melatonin and cortisol secretions before and after subchronic administration of Hyperforat.

AU:Demisch-L, Nispel-J, Sielaff-T, Gebhart-P, Köhler-C, Pflug-B

SO:Abstract from the AGNP-symposium, Nuernberg 1991.

Description

Nocturnal plasma profiles were measured in 12 healthy volunteers before and after 3 weeks of hypericum treatment (Hyperforat, 90 drops/day). They also received light treatment with either 300 or > 2500 lux before and after hypericum treatment. Plasma melatonin and cortisol were measured by immunometric methods.

Results

● Before medication only pulses of 2,500 lux, but not pulses of 300 lux , suppressed melatonin plasma levels.

● After medication light pulses of 300 lux also had a significant effect

● The nocturnal secretion of melatonin increased significantly after medication.

● After three weeks of medication, nocturnal stress stimulation (awakening and sitting) led to a significantly smaller increase in plasma cortisol.

Researchers' conclusion

● Subchronic intake of hypericum changed mechanisms of the visual system associated with the production of melatonin. "Stress" induced nocturnal cortisol secretions may also contribute to a therapeutic effect.

Study 20

Pharmaceutic investigations of the antidepressant effect of *Hypericum perforatum L*

AU: Winterhof-H, Butterweck-V, Nahrstedt-A, Gumbinger-HG, Schulz-V, Erping-S, Bosshamer-F, Wieligmann-A

SO: "Phytopharmaka in Forschung unf klinischer Anwendung" Loew D :1995 Steinkopff Verlag GmbH & Co. KG. Darmstadt S39-52

Basal Temperature

Hypericum extract did raise the basal temperature in mice a statistically significant amount. The effect lasted for more than 4 hours.

The ketamin sleeping time

Hypericum and Buproprion (a dopamine reuptake inhibitor) did shorten ketamin-induced sleeping time in rats; the opposite effect of Imipramine, which lengthened the sleeping time. Hypericin alone was not as effective.

The open field test

Hypericum did not show any unspecific activating effects on male rats in the so-called "open field test" (a test where you measure the spontaneous activity of rats by the amount of lines crossed in a field).

Forced swimming "Porsolt test"

In the so-called "forced swimming" or "Porsolt test" hypericum showed an effect similar to Imipramine on the behavior of mice.

The Porsolt test measures how long mice remain immobile in a stress situation. It can be seen as a way to measure the "fighting spirit" of mice and has previously been proven to be an effective indicator of the antidepressant effect of different pharmaceutical compounds.

In this study it was found that 125 mg of 0.24-0.32% hypericum extract had an effect similar to 10 mg Imipramine on the forced swimming behavior of mice. This indicates that 10 mg of Imipramine could be seen as equivalent to 0.35 mg of total hypericin (0.28 % x 125 mg = 0.35 mg).

Porsolt test together with dopamine blockage

When exposed to the dopamineantagonists Haloperodol (Haldol) and Sulpirid, the effect of hypericum in the Porsolt test was blocked. Rats only given Haloperidol and Sulpirid also performed better. This indicates that dopamine might be of great importance in the effect of hypericum extract.

Effect on dopamine metabolism

Hypericum extract did increase the ratio of homovanillin acid to dopamine in rat brains. This indicates an increased turnover of dopamine as a result of hypericum medication.

Effect on prolactin and cortisol levels

Both serum-cortisol and serum-prolactin were lowered significantly after three weeks of treatment with hypericum extract in male rats. The lowering of prolactin is an indirect indicator of a dopamine effect of hypericum extract, as an increase of dopamine generally leads to a decrease of prolactin and vice versa.

Other Studies

Study 21

Effects of hypericum extract on the sleep EEG in older volunteers

Au: Schulz and M. Jobert

So: J Geriatr Psych in. try Neurol 1994; 7(suppl 1): PP 39-43

Introduction

Sleep is an actively controlled resting state associated with characteristic changes in central nervous activity. The various stages of sleep can be distinguished and the cyclic course of sleep demonstrated with the help of EEGs and other electro-physiologic parameters (electromyogram, EMG; electroocu-logram, EOG). The EEG, EMG, and EOG biosignals can be evaluated either visually or by automated means. It is also possible to differentiate between the non-REM (NREM) stages 1, 2, 3, and 4 of sleep and REM sleep. Due to the marked delta activity in the EEG (slow, high-amplitude waves in the frequency range below 4 Hz) recorded during the NREM stages 3 and 4, these stages are also known as slow-wave sleep.

Depressive illnesses are accompanied by characteristic changes in sleep. Sleep is fitful, and early waking is frequent. Slow-wave sleep can be reduced and the time between sleep onset and the appearance of the first REM sleep in the night (REM latency) is shortened.

An increased activity of cholinergic systems with a simultaneous weakening of aminergic transmitter systems has been postulated as the neurobiologic basis of these changes in sleep structure.

Antidepressants intervene in this process and lead to typical changes in sleep profile. With tricyclic antidepressants, this intervention includes a prolongation of REM latency and a reduction in REM sleep, which can be associated with a marked flattening of the ultradian rhythm (physiological activities that occur more than once every 24 hours).

Description

Twelve older female volunteers with a mean age of 60 years went through two 4-week treatment phases (placebo and active treatment) separated by a washout period of 14 days. Active treatment was given with the hypericum extract LI 160 (Jarsin) in a daily dose of 3 x 0.9 mg hypericin). The 12 subjects were divided into two groups: Group I received LI 160 in the first 4 weeks and a placebo in the second phase, and group II began with the 4 weeks of placebo and was transferred to LI 160 in the second phase.

Each subject spent a total of 4 nights (study days 2, 30, 44, and 72) in the sleep laboratory, when the sleep polygraph was recorded. Each of these nights was preceded by an adaptation night (study days 1, 29, 43, and 71).

Conclusion

The aim of this double-blind study was to investigate the effects of 4 weeks of treatment with hypericum on sleep and well-being. The purpose was to find out whether hypericum's action on sleep is comparable to that of the tricyclic antidepressants and nonselective MAO inhibitors, which cause a prolongation in REM latency and a suppression of REM sleep.

The results show that hypericum has a different profile of action: contrary to the working hypothesis, under active treatment there was actually a slight reduction (on average 10 minutes) in REM sleep latency, whereas under the placebo, the median REM sleep latency remained virtually unchanged. It cannot, however, be ruled out that changes in REM sleep occurred at the start of treatment with hypericum that were not detected when they were measured 4 weeks later.

The proportion of REM sleep in the total sleep period was within the normal range at 20% and was not altered by treatment with hypericum. In the investigated group of older, healthy volunteers, several weeks of treatment with hypericum thus had no effect on the time of appearance or amount of REM sleep.

The observation that the total amount of sleep fell slightly during active treatment and the waking period increased indicates that hypericum does not have any sedative potential, but rather a moderate activating effect on wakefulness. This effect of hypericum can depend, however, both on the dose and the time of ingestion.

Notably, there was an increase in slow-wave sleep in the deep stages 3 and 4 under treatment with hypericum. The baseline value of slow-wave sleep in the subjects was low and amounted on average to less than 5% of the total. This small proportion corresponds to the known reduction in deep sleep with increasing age.

The increase in sleep stages 3 and 4 in the visual evaluation of the sleep EEG corresponded with the increase in slow-wave activity in the automated analysis, which enabled the output in the delta-frequency range to be quantified. This result might be associated with the clinically observed antidepressant effect of LI 160, since several authors assume that a deficit in slow-wave sleep is a significant neurobiologic indicator in affective disorders. Kupfer et al. also reported that the prognosis in patients with depression who had a high proportion of slow-wave activity in the sleep EEG (delta sleep ratio") was considerably more favorable than in those patients with low values. According to the results of the present study, the neurophysiologic activity of LI 160 is displayed more in terms of slow-wave EEG activity than in parameters of REM sleep.

Study 22

Phytotoxicity caused by hypericum

AU:Siegers-C-P, Biel-S, Wilhelm-K-P

So: Nervenheilkunde 12(1993) 320-322

In this study the effect of different hypericum extracts on human keratinocytes radiated with UV-light was investigated.

The results imply that hypericum has no phytotoxic effect in antidepressant doses. Experience from animals and HIV experiments with hypericin indicate that phytotoxic effects might come in light-colored people when exposed to sunlight and a dose of hypericum 30-50 times higher than the antidepressant doses. There were big differences between different hypericum extracts concerning phytotoxicity, as seen in Figure 25.

Study 23

Interaction of hypericum extract and alcohol

AU: Scmidt-U, Harrer-G, Kuhn-K, Berger-Deinert-W, Luther-D

SO: Nervenheilkunde 12 (1993):6: 314-319

The interaction of hypericum with alcohol was investigated in a randomized, double-blind crossover design performed on 32 male and female healthy subjects. One group was given hypericum extract (0.9 mg standard hypericin x 3) for seven days and then a placebo for seven days. The other group was given a placebo for seven days and hypericum for seven days. At days 7 and 14 the subjects were given alcohol so that they reached a blood alcohol level between 0.45 and 0.8 promille. They were then given a series of cognitive and motoric tests in order to see if medication with hypericum would affect the results. There were no significant differences in test results between the placebo and trial groups. It can therefore be concluded that there is no interaction between hypericum and alcohol with respect to cognitive capacities.

There was a slight improvement in results in the hypericum group compared to the placebo group in a test simulating advanced car driving. The difference was not statistically significant.

The hypericum preparation was well tolerated and there was only one case with possible side effects.

Study 24

The influence of St. John's wort on CNS activity

AU: Johnsson-D, Siebenhuener-G, Hofer-E, Sauerwein-Giese-E, Frauendorf-A

SO: TW Neurologishe Psychiatrie 6, 436-444, juni 1992

Effects on auditory and visually evoked potential and EEG were measured in 12 subjects during six weeks' treatment with Jarsin (0.37 mg x 3). After only two weeks, the phases were considerably shortened compared to the baseline values; this reduction reached its greatest extent after four to six weeks (11). This implies improved reaction time when treated with hypericum extract.

The subjects' ability to perform an attention test and the so-called Mackworth Clock (another cognitive attention test) showed statistically verified better results after treatment with hypericum.

The EEGs showed a typical antidepressant profile with an increase of theta and beta frequencies and a decrease in alpha frequencies.

The well-being scale showed a slightly better result in the trial group compared to the placebo group, although the subjects were not depressed or sick at the start of the study. There were no significant differences between hypericum and the placebo concerning self-rated judgement of effect.

The authors concluded that hypericum seems to have an activating effect on cognitive perception and reaction time and that it has no sedating effects. They compare the effect to that of Imipramine in the so-called Kielholz schedule, a schedule that classifies the different classic antidepressants regarding activating, antidepressive and sedating effects. See Figure 15.

Figure 15. Hypericums place in the "Kielholz schedule".

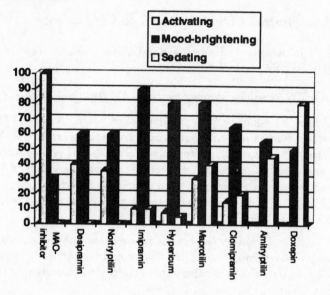

Study 25

Effect of hypericum extract LI 160 compared with Maprotiline on resting EEG and evoked potentials in 24 volunteers

AU: Johnson-D, Ksciuk-H, Woelk-H, Sauerwein-Giese-E, Frauendorf-A

J Geriatrric Psychiatry Neur 1994; 7 (Suppl 1). S44-S46

The effects of hypericum extract were compared with those of Maprotiline in a randomized, double-blind study in 24 healthy subjects. The investigations were based on measurements of the resting EEG and on visual and auditory evoked potentials. In the resting EEG, the two medications caused opposite changes in the theta region, but predominantly uniform changes in the alpha and beta regions. Measurements of evoked potentials in the theta and beta regions supported these findings. Overall, the results suggested improvements in cognitive function and also of relaxant properties, especially with the hypericum extract.

Study 26

The use of an infusion of St. John's wort in the combined treatment of alcoholics with peptic ulcer and chronic gastritis

AU: Krylov-AA; Ibatov-AN

SO: Vrach-Delo. 1993 Feb-Mar (2-3): 146-8

Summary

Hypericum herbal infusion was used in combination with rational psychotherapy of depressive manifestations in 57 outpatients with alcoholism and concomitant diseases of digestive organs. Duration of treatment—2 months (1 glass 4-5 times daily). It is concluded that this treatment in combination with rational psychotherapy proved effective.

Clinical, Criteria-Based Reviews

Study 27

St. John's Wort as antidepressive therapy

AU - Ernst ESO - Fortschritte der Medizin 1995 Sep 10;113(25):354-5

Study search

A computerized medical search from 1980 through 1994 was made in order to find all randomized clinical trials on the antidepressant effect of hypericum. In addition, all manufacturers of hypericum preparations were asked to contribute published and unpublished material. The references of the studies included were also retrieved in order to not miss anything of importance.

Inclusion criteria

Studies had to score 40 points or more out of 110 possible on a criteria-based evaluation score to be included. The evaluation score was an extended and modified version of the one published by Kleijnen et al. in 1991.

Table 18 gives a brief description of these criteria.

Criterion	points given
required sample size compared to pre-calculated sample size (One point per 10 study participants)	10
Study population adequately described	10
Random procedure described and adequate	10
Double blinding (Placebo and active substance indistinguishable)	10
compliance tested	10
endpoint relevant (tested instrument)	10
results described so that they can be checked	10
information regarding dropouts given	10
information on ADR provided	10
intent to treat analysis performed	10

Fourteen studies comparing hypericum with a placebo were found. Nine of these scored more than 40 points and were thus included in the continuing evaluation.

Four trials were identified where hypericum monopreparations were tested against reference medications. Three of them scored more than 40 points. Thus, twelve studies qualified for further review

Authors' comments

Hypericum is effective

The results of this review imply that hypericum is effective in alleviating the symptoms of a variety of depressive disorders. Only two studies conducted against a placebo contradict this notion (Lehr and Woelk 1993, Osterheider et al. 1992). One (Osterheider) was published as an abstract only (thus essential details are lacking for a meaningful interpretation), and both failed to receive a quality rating high enough for inclusion in this review. Thus, almost all placebo-controlled studies reviewed above demonstrate that hypericum is superior to a placebo in treating depression.

The studies conducted against standard antidepressants suggest that the therapeutic effect of hypericum is similar to that of Imipramine or Maprotiline. Taken together, these data are scientifically compelling and leave little doubt as to the efficacy of hypericum in the treatment of depressive symptoms.

Criticism

Some critical points ought to be raised. Most of the studies have been published recently, virtually all in German and many in journals that might be unfamiliar to an international audience. Phytomedicine has clearly more of a domain on the Continent than in Britain or the US; the money annually spent on the Continent per capita on prescribed herbal monopreparations, for instance, is one order of magnitude more than in the UK (De Smet 1993).

Thus it is understandable that much of the literature relating to this topic should be published in German journals. Publication bias might have distorted the overall picture. However, there is no definite evidence to suggest that it has, in effect, taken place.

Few ADRs

One of the possible strengths of phytomedicines is the relative lack of ADRs (Ernst 1995). With antidepressants suicides through overdose represent a particular problem (Jick et al. 1995). There are no reports of hypericum intoxication, but the overall death rate following overdose of synthetic antidepressants has recently been reported to amount to 30.1 deaths per million prescriptions (Henry et al. 1995). It is conceivable that hypericum offers a relevant advantage over conventional antidepressants in this respect. More research is needed if this notion is to be developed into evidence.

Too good to be true?

Another relevant concern is the heterogeneity of diagnoses. According to the evidence presented here, hypericum seems to be effective for almost any type of depression. This may be correct, but to many it will sound "too good to be true." Further work needs to address this question and should attempt to determine which diagnostic entities (types of depression) are optimally amenable to treatment with hypericum and which are not.

About the Authors

HAROLD H. BLOOMFIELD, M.D. is a Yale-trained psychiatrist and one of the leading psychological educators of our time.

Dr. Bloomfield's first book, *TM-Transcendental Meditation*, was an international bestseller on the New York *Times* list for over 6 months. Dr. Bloomfield's other bestsellers, *How To Survive the Loss of a Love* (over 2 million copies sold) and *How to Heal Depression* have become self-help classics. His other works, *Making Peace With Your Parents*, *Making Peace With Yourself*, *Lifemates*, and *Making Peace in Your Stepfamily*, introduced personal, marital, and family peacemaking to millions of people.

Dr. Bloomfield's books have sold over six million copies and have been translated into twenty-four languages. His newest books are *The Power of 5*, and *How to Feel Safe in an Unsafe World*.

Dr. Bloomfield has frequently appeared on "The Oprah Winfrey Show," "Sally Jessy Raphael," "Larry King," 'Geraldo,'" and "Good Morning America." In addition to professional journals, his work and popular articles appear in *USA Today, Los Angeles Times*, San Francisco *Examiner, Newsweek, Cosmopolitan, Ladies' Home Journal, New Woman, American Health* and *Prevention*.

Dr. Bloomfield has received the Medical Self-Care Magazine Book-of-the-Year Award, The Golden Apple Award for Outstanding Psychological Educator, and the American Holistic Health Association's Lifetime Achievement Award. He is an adjunct professor of psychology at the Union Graduate School and a member of the American Psychiatric Association and the San Diego Psychiatric Society.

Dr. Bloomfield is a much-admired keynote speaker for public programs, corporate meetings, and professional conferences.

Dr. Bloomfield maintains a private practice of psychiatry, psychotherapy, and executive counseling in Del Mar, California.

Harold H. Bloomfield, M.D.
1337 Camino Del Mar
Del Mar, California 90014
619-481-9950 (phone)
619-792-2333 (fax)

MIKAEL NORDFORS, M.D., is a psychiatric researcher at Sahlgrehnska University Hospital in Gothenburg, Sweden. His medical knowledge, research skills, and fluency in several languages have been invaluable in tracking down, translating, and understanding the medical studies on hypericum.

PETER MCWILLIAMS is a writer and video author. His books include *How to Heal Depression* (with Dr. Bloomfield), *How to Survive the Loss of a Love* (with Dr. Bloomfield and Melba Colgrove, Ph.D.), *You Can't Afford the Luxury of a Negative Thought*, *DO IT!*, *LIFE 101*, and *Ain't Nobody's Business if You Do*. His home page, where the complete text of most of his books are available, is

http://www.mcwilliams.com.

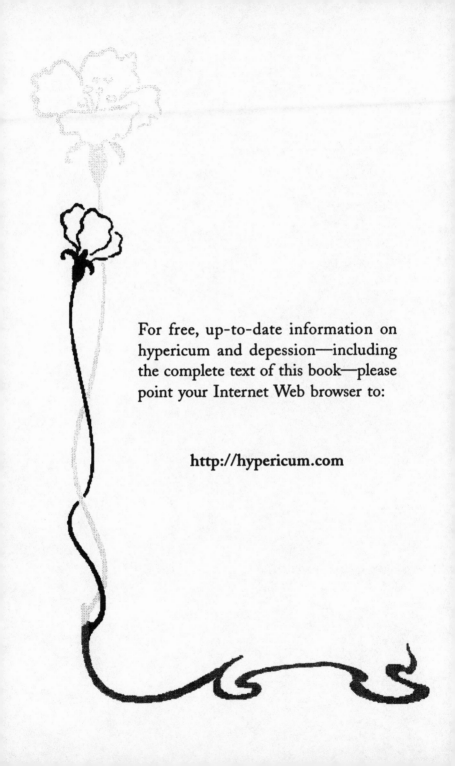

For free, up-to-date information on hypericum and depession—including the complete text of this book—please point your Internet Web browser to:

http://hypericum.com

For a free Prelude Press catalog or to order additional copies of this book, please call:

800-LIFE-101

(800-543-3101)